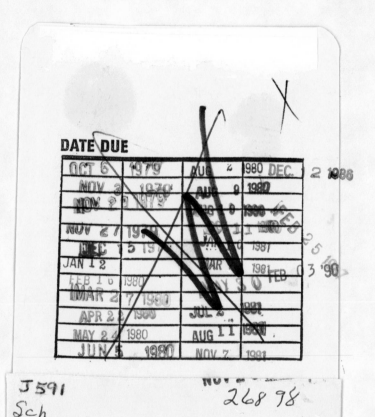

Charlie Brown's
Super Book of
Questions and Answers

about all kinds of animals...from snails to people!

Charlie Brown's Super Book of Questions and Answers

about all kinds of animals... from snails to people!

Based on the Charles M. Schulz Characters

Random House New York

Art Director: Eleanor Ehrhardt
Designer: Terry Flanagan
Typography: Charlotte Staub

Editor: Hedda Nussbaum

Special thanks to:

Barbara Neill
Senior Instructor
Alexander M. White Natural Science Center
Museum of Natural History, New York

Dr. Fleur Strand
Professor of Biology
New York University

Copyright © 1976 by United Feature Syndicate, Inc. Produced in association with Charles M. Schulz Creative Associates, Warren Lockhart, President. All rights reserved under International and Pan-American Copyright Conventions. Published in the United States by Random House, Inc., New York, and simultaneously in Canada by Random House of Canada Limited, Toronto. Library of Congress Cataloging in Publication Data. Charlie Brown's super book of questions and answers about all kinds of animals . . . from snails to people! Summary: Charlie Brown and the rest of the Peanuts gang help present hundreds of scientific facts about the animal kingdom in a question and answer format. 1. Animals—Miscellanea—Juvenile literature. 2. Human biology—Miscellanea—Juvenile literature. 1. Animals—Miscellanea. 2. Human biology. 3. Questions and answers. I. Schulz, Charles M. QL49.C475 J591 76-2068
ISBN 0-394-83249-3/0-394-93249-8 (lib. bdg.) Manufactured in the United States of America   4 5 6 7 8 9 0
Grateful acknowledgment is made to Follett Publishing Company for permission to reprint the illustrations on pages 6, 10, 13, 15, 35, 44, 45, 52, 58, 66, 75, 92, reprinted from *Science for Human Value*. Copyright © 1972 by Follett Publishing Company.

Introduction

Do you ever ask questions? Of course! Everyone does. Questions are easy to ask. But sometimes the answers are hard to find.

Now the Peanuts gang is here to help you. In this book you will find out all kinds of things about all kinds of animals—from snails to people. That means you'll find the answer to "Why does a dog wag its tail?" and to "Why does your mouth water when you smell food?" and to "Where does the tadpole's tail go when the tadpole becomes a frog?" and to many, many, many more questions.

So join Charlie Brown and start asking some questions!

Contents

About the Animal Kingdom

How many different kinds of animals are there?

No! There are a lot more than that. More than one million kinds of animals live on the earth. When we think of animals, we usually think of our pets, the animals on a farm, and the animals in a zoo. We forget the creatures that live in the ocean. We forget insects, worms, and spiders. We even forget birds. They are all animals, too.

To a scientist, an animal is anything that is alive but is not a plant. The list of animals includes creatures that are so tiny we can see them only under a microscope. And the list includes you, too!

How smart are animals?

No other animals are as smart as people. But some are very intelligent. Apes, monkeys, and dolphins are the smartest. They can learn to do many things. Some of them can even solve problems. For example, a dolphin in a tank was once playing catch with a feather. One time the feather stuck to the side of the tank, high above the water. The game seemed to be over. But the dolphin figured out how to get the feather back. It jumped up and brushed the feather loose with the side of its head. The dolphin had solved its problem, and the game could go on. Most animals are not nearly this smart. Animals such as clams, crabs, insects, and worms are the least intelligent of all. They can't learn to do very much. Some can't learn anything.

What are instincts?

Animals are born knowing how to do certain things. A bird is born knowing how to build a nest. A fish is born knowing how to swim. A spider is born knowing how to spin a web. No one has to teach the animals to do these things. We say that the animals have an instinct for doing them. Instincts are not a sign of intelligence. When an animal acts from instinct, it does not have to learn anything or solve a problem.

Do animals talk to each other?

Yes, animals do talk to each other, but with "animal talk," not human talk. Animals do not use words and sentences the way people do. They express ideas and feelings to each other by using movements, smells, and sounds. A honeybee does a kind of dance to tell other honeybees where to find nectar. A female wolf gives off a certain smell that tells a male wolf she is ready to mate. A kitten meows to its mother to let her know it is hungry. A bird sings to warn other birds to keep away from its nest. These are all ways that animals talk to each other. Another animal of the same kind will understand the feeling or idea being expressed.

Some scientists think that dolphins may be able to talk the way humans do. But so far no one has proved that they can.

You can sometimes hear a lion's roar ten miles away!

How long do animals live?

The longest-living animal is probably the tortoise. We think it may live more than 150 years. At the other extreme is the mayfly, which lives only a few hours. The other animals are in between. An elephant can live 60 or 70 years. Your dog or cat will live about 12 or 15 years. A rat or mouse will live only 2 or 3 years. Some people say there are parrots that have lived more than 100 years, but no one has proved they do. Parrots can probably live about 50 years. So can geese, swans, and alligators. Rattlesnakes can live up to 18 years, but garter snakes don't usually live more than 5 or 6 years. People live about as long as elephants—around 70 years.

I DON'T SEE ANY GRAY HAIRS!

What is the biggest animal?

The biggest animal in the world is the blue whale. Some blue whales have grown as long as 109 feet and have weighed 150 tons!

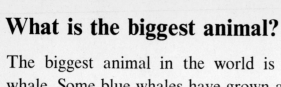

A baby whale gains about 200 pounds a day

Why do some animals sleep all winter?

Many animals—such as the woodchuck—sleep all winter because they can't find food then. The plants that they eat die or lose their leaves when the weather gets cold. These animals eat a lot before winter comes, and grow fat. Then they sleep—or hibernate—inside a deep hole. They live all winter on the fat stored in their bodies. When spring comes, warmth and hunger wake up the sleepers.

Other animals, such as snakes, hibernate to escape cold weather. When the temperature is low, these animals slow down and can hardly move at all. If they stayed outside, they would freeze. So they spend the winter sleeping in a protected place.

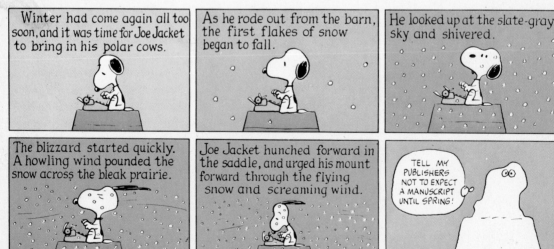

4

What animals sleep all winter?

The winter sleepers include the ground squirrels, woodchucks, some bats, and jumping mice. Other animals, such as the bear, skunk, chipmunk, and badger, sleep part of the winter. They come out on days when the air isn't very cold. Many toads, turtles, snakes, frogs, and salamanders and some insects also hibernate.

What is the fastest animal?

The fastest of all animals is a bird called the swift. The spine-tailed swift can fly at a speed of more than 100 miles an hour. The word "swift" means fast, so there's no question about how this bird got its name.

The fastest land animal is the cheetah. It can run at more than 60 miles an hour.

How do animals live in the desert?

A desert is a very dry place. Animals that live there cannot always find water. But many small desert animals don't have to drink any water. They get all they need by eating desert plants. These plants have water stored in them.

During the day, most desert animals stay underground or in the shade. The hot sun would make them sweat. They would lose much of the water in their bodies. Instead, these animals come out at night, when the desert is cool. Then they don't sweat.

The camel gets along in another way. The camel must drink water. But once it has drunk, it can go for days without drinking any more. Its body is made especially for storing a lot of water. The camel can stay out in the hot sun because it sweats very little. So it does not lose the water stored in its body.

How do mother animals know their own babies?

By their smell. When a baby animal is born, its mother sniffs it and remembers the smell. From then on, whenever the mother wants to find her baby, she will sniff all the babies around until she finds the right one.

What are tails for?

The tails of animals are good for many things. A cow uses its tail as a fly swatter when it swishes away pesty insects. A fox wraps itself up in its tail to keep warm. A beaver slaps its flat tail on the water to give a warning signal. A fish uses its tail to help it swim. A squirrel uses its tail as a parachute when it jumps through treetops. A spider monkey can wrap its tail around a branch, and swing.

 A lizard called the gecko can drop its tail and grow a new one!

Why are there zoos?

Zoos were started so that people could see animals from strange, faraway places. Many people would never see zebras, elephants, peacocks, emus, and gnus if there were no zoos. Today we have zoos for other reasons, too. We keep them as places to raise and protect animals that are dying out.

Why do some animals die out?

In the past 200 years people have caused many kinds of animals to die out—to become extinct. People keep building houses and factories in fields and woods. As they spread over the land, they destroy animals' homes. If the animals can't find a place to live, they die out. Sixteen kinds of Hawaiian birds have become extinct for this reason. Other animals, such as the Florida Key deer, may soon die out because they are losing their homes. Hunters have caused some animals to become extinct, too. In the last century, hunters killed all the passenger pigeons in North America and most of the buffaloes. Today they are fast killing off hawks and wolves.

Pollution is killing many animals today, too. As rivers become polluted, fish are poisoned. Many die. Birds that eat the poisoned fish can't lay strong, healthy eggs. New birds aren't born. So far, no kinds of animals have become extinct because of pollution. But some, such as the bald eagle and the brown pelican, have become rare and may die out.

Scientists think that some animals become extinct because of changes in climate. The places where they live become hotter or cooler, drier or wetter. The food that they usually eat cannot grow there any more. If the animals can't learn to eat something else, they die. Dinosaurs may have died out for this reason.

BALD EAGLE

DINOSAUR.

Animals with No Bones

Are there animals that don't have any bones?

Yes. Insects, worms, and many animals that live in the sea have no bones. Most of these animals do have some hard parts. But these parts are on the outside of their bodies. The hard parts protect the animals' soft insides.

What are sea shells?

Sea shells are the hard, protective cases that certain sea animals form around themselves. Oysters, mussels, clams, scallops, and snails are all animals that have shells.

The sea shells you find sometimes have living animals inside. But usually the shells are empty by the time you get to them. The animals have been eaten by other sea animals or by sea gulls. The shells are often pretty, and it's fun to take them home.

Can you hear the sea in a sea shell?

No, you can't. When you hold a large spiral-shaped shell to your ear, you hear a roar. But it's not the roar of the sea. The shape of the shell makes any slight sound in the air echo back and forth inside the shell. Sounds that you may not normally hear are picked up by the shell and made louder.

The shell of a giant clam may weigh up to 600 pounds!

How does an oyster make a pearl?

Sometimes a little grain of sand gets inside the shell of a pearl oyster. The sand rubs against the soft body of the oyster. To stop the rubbing, the oyster wraps the sand in layer after layer of the same shiny coating it makes to line its shell. We call this coating mother-of-pearl. Gradually the bit of sand is wrapped in so many layers that a little ball forms. This ball is a pearl.

What happens if you grab a crab by one leg?

If the crab doesn't pinch you, it will probably let its leg drop off! The crab will run away, and you will be left holding the leg in your hand. Dropping a leg is the crab's way of protecting itself from you or any other danger. The crab can easily grow a new leg to replace the one it left behind.

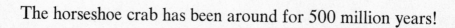

! The horseshoe crab has been around for 500 million years! **!**

What is a sponge?

A sponge is a sea animal with a soft, elastic skeleton. The animal has no legs, arms, fins, or stomach, and it doesn't move around at all. For many years people thought the sponge was really a plant. The soft skeleton of a dead sponge can hold a lot of water, so people have long used sponges for cleaning. But today, the sponge you use to wipe your kitchen counter is probably made in a factory.

Why does an octopus squirt black ink into the water?

An octopus squirts black ink into the water in order to hide from an enemy. That enemy may be a shark, a whale, or a person.

What does an octopus do with its eight arms?

An octopus uses its eight arms to catch crabs, clams, lobsters, and other shellfish. It also uses its arms to break open their shells, so it can eat them. On the underside of each arm are round muscles that act like suction cups. They can hold onto anything the octopus catches.

Why do jellyfish sting?

Jellyfish sting in order to get food. A jellyfish is a sea animal with a soft body and no shell. It eats other sea animals. First it paralyzes a small animal with its sting. Because the animal cannot move, the jellyfish can grab it and eat it. When you are swimming in the ocean, you may bump into a jellyfish and get stung. The sting may hurt, but you won't be paralyzed. So don't worry—the jellyfish will never eat *you*!

What sea animal looks like a flower?

The sea anemone (uh-NEM-uh-nee) looks like a flower, or at least like some sort of plant. It is a simple animal—just a hollow tube with a mouth at one end and a lot of wavy "arms" around the mouth. The arms are used to capture food. Sea anemones come in a variety of colors—red, green, brown, and orange. Some have dots and some have stripes.

Can you eat a sea cucumber?

Yes, but it doesn't taste like the cucumber you eat in a salad. A sea cucumber is not a vegetable. It is an animal that lives in the sand at the bottom of the sea. It was named "sea cucumber" because it is long and thin and looks much like a cucumber. However, it changes its shape all the time as it moves around. Sometimes it is very long and very skinny. Sometimes it is short and fat. Sometimes it is fat at both ends and skinny in the middle. Sea cucumbers are used in Oriental cooking. You can find them on the menu in some Chinese restaurants.

How do snails walk?

Snails have no legs, but they do have a foot. The whole bottom part of a snail's body is one smooth, flat foot. It moves the snail along the ground. As the snail moves, its foot gives off a slimy liquid. The liquid helps the snail to move more easily.

If you cut a starfish in pieces, each piece will grow into a whole starfish!

What happens to an earthworm when it is cut in two?

You might expect that the worm would die, but it doesn't always. A worm's body is one long row of sections that are all pretty much the same. A worm can lose a few of these sections without dying.

When a worm is cut into two pieces, the pieces wiggle around for a while. But they do not become two separate worms. The smaller piece usually dies. The larger piece can usually grow back the sections it lost—if it lost just a few.

VERY INTERESTING!

A WORM TWO FEET LONG? THAT'S RIDICULOUS!

How long was the longest earthworm ever found?

The longest earthworm was even longer than two feet. It was nine feet long!

Insects

How many insects are there in the world?

A lot! Scientists say that there are about as many insects in one square mile of fertile land as there are people on the whole earth. So just think how many insects there might be in 100 square miles, in 1,000 square miles, and in the entire world!

What is an insect?

An insect is a very small animal with six legs. Many insects have two feelers and four wings, but others don't. There are many, many thousands of kinds of insects. They all look a little different. Such animals as flies, ants, bees, cockroaches, beetles, crickets, and butterflies are insects.

Where do all the insects come from?

They come from eggs. Female insects lay hundreds or even thousands of eggs during their lives. For example, a queen bee does nothing all summer but lay eggs. On any one day she may lay as many as 1,500. A female termite lays even more. She can lay as many as 30,000 eggs in one day!

If every insect hatched and lived its full life, the world would be over-run with insects. There would be no room for anyone else. Fortunately for us, many animals eat insects and insect eggs. Most insects never have a chance to grow up.

! Three hundred babies come out of each egg laid by a chalcid fly wasp! !

Are insects of any use to us?

Some insects are very useful to us. Bees make honey. Silkworms make silk, which we use for clothing. An insect called the lac gives off a sticky liquid that we use to make shellac. Bees, butterflies, moths, and other insects carry the yellow dust called pollen from flower to flower. Then the plants can grow seeds, which will become new plants. We eat some of these seeds in fruits and vege-tables, and we plant some seeds for new crops.

There are also many harmful insects that spread disease, damage plants, and eat clothing and furniture. And there are insects, such as the mosquito, that bite us. But other insects help to get rid of these harmful ones. For example, the praying mantis and the ladybug eat large numbers of harmful insects.

Why are insects so thin?

Insects are very thin because of the way they breathe. They have no lungs for breathing air. Instead, they breathe air through tiny holes in their bodies. The air cannot travel very far through these holes. If an insect were fat, air could not reach every part of its body. The insect could not live. So, in order to get air into all parts of their bodies, insects must be very skinny.

What was the largest insect ever to live?

Many millions of years ago there lived a giant dragonfly whose body was 15 inches long. Its wings measured more than 27 inches from the tip of one wing to the tip of another. However, this insect's body was only about a quarter of an inch thick. If the dragonfly had been fatter, it would not have been able to breathe.

IT'S A BIRD!
IT'S THE RED BARON!!
IT'S A DRAGONFLY!!!

What is the largest insect living today?

The largest insect is a type of "walking stick" that lives in the tropics. It is very long and skinny, and it looks a lot like a twig when it rests on a tree. This walking stick sometimes grows to be nearly 13 inches long.

Where do insects go in winter?

Most insects die at the end of the summer. But they leave many eggs to hatch in the spring. Bumblebees die, but they don't leave eggs. Instead, their queen stays alive all winter. She sleeps underground until spring. Then she comes out and starts laying eggs. Other insects also stay alive during the winter. These sleep underground or in a barn or cellar for the winter months. Crickets and mosquitoes do this. Ants do, too. But ants come out on warm, sunny winter days. Monarch butterflies are like birds. They fly south to warmer places for the winter.

Some monarch butterflies travel more than 2,000 miles to the south for the winter!

What insects act the most like people?

Ants act the most like people. They live in nests that are much like cities. Often the nests are built underground and are full of tunnels. They may have roads leading to and from the entrance. Inside the city, ants keep busy doing different jobs. Some clean the tunnels, some take care of babies, and some guard the city. Others go outside and gather food.

There are ants that fight wars. There are ants that have slaves. There are even ants that keep other insects as pets. Some kinds of ants grow their own food in gardens. Others keep "ant cows."

What is an "ant cow"?

An ant cow is another name for an insect called an aphid (AY-fid). Aphids make a sweet liquid called honeydew. Certain kinds of ants keep aphids and "milk" them, just as farmers keep cows. An ant farmer uses its feelers to stroke an aphid's sides. The aphid then lets out a drop of honeydew for the ant to drink.

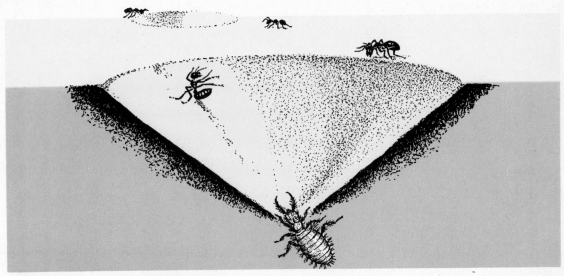

What is a doodlebug?

A doodlebug is another name for a young antlion. An antlion is not an ant and it's not a lion. It is an insect that—to an ant—might seem as ferocious as a lion seems to us.

In the early part of its life, an antlion digs a pit in sand and buries itself at the bottom. Only its head sticks out. It waits for an ant to fall into the pit. When one does, the antlion kills it and sucks the juices out of its body.

Are ladybugs useful?

Yes, ladybugs are very useful because they eat aphids. Although ants like aphids, people don't. Aphids drink the juices in plants and ruin farmers' crops. Ladybugs eat so many aphids that people use them to control the pests. Some farmers raise ladybugs and let them go in places where aphids are eating the crops.

19

How can a fly walk on the ceiling?

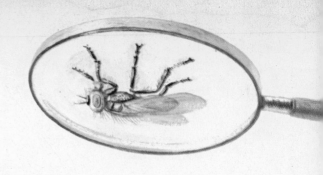

A fly can walk upside down on the ceiling because of the pads on each of its six feet. If you look at a fly with a magnifying glass, you can see these pads clearly. Some scientists think that the fly stays on the ceiling because the pads are sticky. Others believe that the curved pads flatten out against the ceiling and hold on the way suction cups do.

Will "darning needles" harm you?

"Darning needles" look like dangerous insects. But they are really perfectly harmless. In fact, they are very helpful to us. They eat many insect pests, such as flies and mosquitoes. A darning needle's real name is dragonfly.

A dragonfly can keep up with a car moving at 50 miles an hour!

How do fireflies light up?

Fireflies make two special juices in their bodies. When these juices mix together with air, fireflies light up. Scientists are not sure why fireflies make this light. But they think that it is probably a signal to attract a mate.

How do bees make honey?

Only one kind of bee—the honeybee—makes honey. First a honeybee goes to flowers to get nectar. Nectar is a sweet liquid found inside the flowers. A bee drinks the nectar and stores it in its "honey stomach." The honey stomach is not the same stomach that the bee uses to digest its food. It is a special stomach where the nectar is changed into watery honey.

The bee then flies back to its hive. It sucks up the watery honey from its honey stomach, and places the honey in little cubbyholes called cells. In the cells, the water dries out of the honey. At last the honey is finished.

21

One thousand bees must work their entire lives to make one pound of honey!

Why do bees buzz?

The sound of a bee buzzing is nothing more than the sound of its wings moving. So when a bee flies, you hear the buzzzzz.

Why do bees sting?

Answer: Bees sting because they are mean. That is why bees sting.

Sally is wrong. Bees are not mean. Bees sting in order to protect themselves from enemies. If you don't bother a bee, it will usually not feel threatened by you, and it will not sting you. However, the smell of certain perfumes may cause a bee to sting. So if you are wearing perfume, watch out!

Does a bee die when it stings you?

Only honeybees die when they sting you. No other bees do. Most of the bees that sting have smooth stingers. After one of them stings you, its stinger slips right out of your flesh. But the honeybee's stinger has a hook at the end of it. When the honeybee flies away after stinging you, the stinger stays hooked into your flesh. Soft parts of the bee's body pull off with the stinger. The honeybee soon dies.

How dangerous is the sting of a bee or a wasp?

The sting of a bee or wasp is usually not dangerous to people. Most of the time the sting hurts a lot, and the area around the sting swells up. But after a while the pain goes away, and so does the swelling. Some people, however, are allergic to the sting. They may break out in a rash, or their eyes and lips may swell up. A few people are so allergic to stings that they have trouble breathing and must quickly see a doctor. This extra strong reaction is not very common.

IGNORE THEM, LINUS. THEY DON'T EVEN LIKE PEANUT BUTTER.

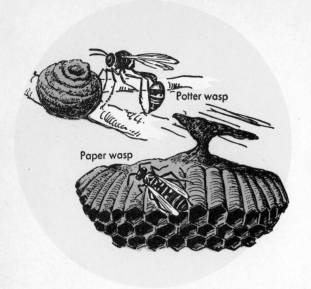

Potter wasp

Paper wasp

What are hornets and yellowjackets?

Hornets and yellowjackets are two of the most familiar kinds of wasps. As wasps, they are related to bees, and are known for their love of fruit juices and their painful stings. Some kinds of wasps live all alone. Others, including hornets and yellowjackets, live in groups as honeybees do. Like all wasps, hornets and yellowjackets are helpful insects. The adults feed their babies insects that are harmful to people and crops.

What is a wasp's nest made of?

Different kinds of wasps make different kinds of nests. Paper wasps, including hornets and yellowjackets, build their nests of paper. They make the paper by chewing up wood. Some wasps make their nests from mud. Mud daubers build rows of mud cells in protected places, such as under bridges and roofs of buildings. Potter wasps attach their mud nests to plants. Theirs look just like tiny clay pots! Carpenter wasps dig tunnels in wood for their nests. Digger wasps dig tunnels in the ground.

Why do mosquito bites itch?

If your mosquito bites itch, you must be allergic to the liquid the mosquito puts under your skin. Only female mosquitoes bite. When one bites you, she pricks your skin with a long, thin part of her mouth. Then she sucks some of your blood for food. The mosquito has a special liquid in her mouth to keep your blood thin and easy to suck. Some of this liquid gets under your skin. It causes the bite to swell and itch—but only if you are allergic to the liquid. Some lucky people are not allergic and never itch at all from mosquito bites!

How did the praying mantis get its name?

When a praying mantis holds its front legs up together, it looks as if it is praying. However, this insect is not praying at all. It is waiting for a smaller insect to come by, so that it can grab the insect with its front legs. The praying mantis will crush the insect and eat it. People like the praying mantis because it eats many insects that harm our crops and carry diseases.

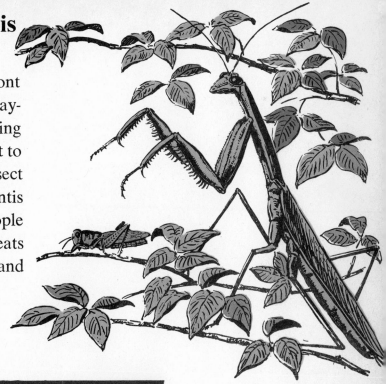

GOOD GRIEF, I WISH MY PRAYING MANTIS WOULD CATCH THAT NOISY MOSQUITO.

Some people tie praying mantises to their beds to catch pesty insects!

What is the difference between a moth and a butterfly?

Moths usually fly at night and butterflies fly during the day. The body of a moth is thick and hairy. The body of a butterfly is thin and not at all hairy. The feelers of a butterfly are slender and have little knobs at the ends. The moth's feelers don't have these knobs, and they are often quite feathery. Both moths and butterflies can be beautifully colored, but butterflies' colors are brighter.

How does a caterpillar turn into a butterfly?

When a butterfly egg hatches, out comes a wormlike creature called a caterpillar. The caterpillar eats a lot of food and grows big. Then it attaches itself to a twig and grows a hard skin. Now it is called a chrysalis (KRIS-uh-lis). For weeks, or sometimes months, the chrysalis stays very still. But inside the hard covering, many changes are slowly taking place. Four wings, six legs, feelers, and new and different eyes are forming. Spring comes, and the covering splits open. A butterfly with tiny damp wings comes out. It hangs on a twig until its wings dry out. Then it is ready to fly away.

Don't butterflies spin cocoons?

No, butterflies do not spin cocoons. But moths do. When a moth caterpillar is big enough, it spins a protective case around itself. This case is called a cocoon. The cocoon is spun of silk, which the caterpillar makes in its body. The caterpillar rests inside its cocoon and slowly changes into a moth. Then, like the butterfly, the moth comes out of its covering and soon flies away.

COCOON

27

Silkworm moth and eggs

Young silkworms

Silkworms spinning cocoons

Open cocoon

How do we get silk from silkworms?

The silkworm is really a caterpillar that will someday become a small pale-gray moth. It spins a cocoon of silk just as other moth caterpillars do. But its silk is especially fine.

The silkworm's silk comes out of its mouth as a thread of gluey liquid. The thread hardens as soon as it touches the air. The thread is often as long as 1,000 feet! The caterpillar winds the thread around and around its body to form a cocoon.

To get the silk, people heat the cocoon and kill the animal inside. Next they put the cocoon in warm water to soften the gum that holds the threads in place. Then they can unwind the thread. From the thread, fine silk material is woven.

WOODSTOCK WOULD HAVE MADE A LOUSY MOTH!

Why do moths gather around light bulbs at night?

Many insects are attracted to light. They have an instinct to go toward it. A moth is one of these insects. When a light goes on, a moth is drawn to it. The moth can't stay away. Since moths are awake at night, you will often see a group of them flying around and around a light bulb.

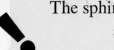 The sphinx moth curls up its long tongue and uses it as a pillow!

Why do moths eat your clothes?

Actually, moths don't eat your clothes. Certain moth caterpillars eat them. Clothes are their food. They especially like wool and fur. These caterpillars get into your closet or drawer if a female moth lays her eggs there. When the eggs hatch, the hungry little caterpillars come out and go to work on your clothes.

How do worms get into apples?

They are born there! In the middle of summer, when apples are growing on apple trees, female flies lay their eggs inside some of the apples. The eggs hatch into tiny worms called larvae (LAR-vee), which begin eating the apples. If you bite into one of these apples, you will find a worm. If no one picks the apples, they fall off the trees in the autumn. The larvae crawl out and bury themselves in the ground. A hard skin forms around each one. The next summer, a fly comes out of the skin.

How do crickets chirp?

Crickets don't use their mouths or throats to make their chirping sound. They rub their wings together. Only male crickets make this sound. They attract female crickets with it.

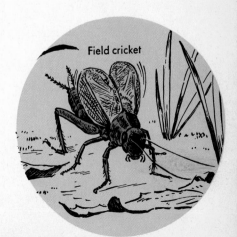

Field cricket

Why do termites eat the frames of our houses?

Termites don't eat the wooden frames of houses just because they are hungry. They are also building their homes in the wood. They chew holes that they use as rooms to live in. They line the holes with chewed-up wood that they have made into a kind of clay.

Wood-eating termites damage more than the frames of houses. They eat wooden bridges, fences, and boats. If they get inside houses, they eat furniture, books, and paper. Look what termites did to Snoopy's house!

Tiny, tiny animals live inside every termite and help it digest wood!

Why can't we get rid of cockroaches?

Cockroaches are experts at staying alive. They can eat almost anything—garbage, soap, book bindings, even television wires! They have been around since the days of the dinosaurs — many millions of years. For a long time, people have been trying to kill off cockroaches because they bring germs into homes and restaurants. Although it is possible to get rid of them for a while, they usually return. Poisons kill cockroaches, but cockroach babies are often born immune to the same poison that killed their parents. This means that the babies cannot be killed by that poison.

Cockroaches like damp and dirty places best. So a clean, dry house may discourage them from coming in. However, they will probably be around somewhere for the next few million years.

Are spiders insects?

Spider

No, spiders are not insects, although they are close relatives. Insects have six legs. Spiders have eight. An insect's body has three main parts. A spider's body has only two. Most insects have feelers and wings. Spiders don't have either. Spiders belong to the group of animals called arachnids (uh-RACK-nids).

Insect

How does a spider spin a web?

A spider spins a web out of silk that it makes inside its body. The silk comes out in very thin liquid threads. As soon as a thread touches air, it hardens. Some of the threads are sticky and some are not. The spider attaches the threads to a tree or house in a particular pattern. One kind of web you may have seen is called an orb web. It looks something like a wheel. Flies and other insects get caught in the sticky threads of the "wheel." The spider then kills the insects and eats them.

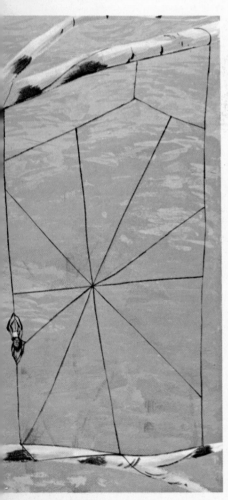
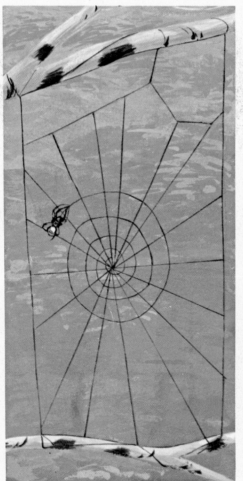
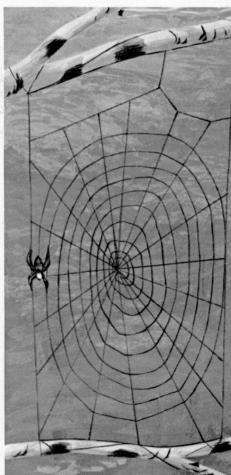

Why aren't spiders caught in their own webs?

A spider is careful to walk only on the non-sticky threads of its web. But even if it does slip and touch the sticky threads, it isn't caught. It is protected by an oily covering on its body.

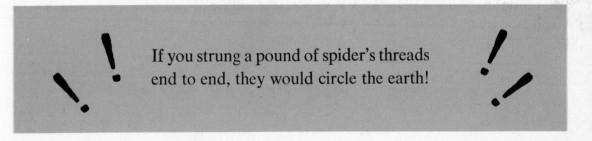

If you strung a pound of spider's threads end to end, they would circle the earth!

What is a daddy-longlegs?

A daddy-longlegs is a relative of the spider, but it does not spin a web. You can easily recognize a daddy-longlegs by its tiny body and eight very long, skinny legs. If it loses one of these legs, it will grow a new one!

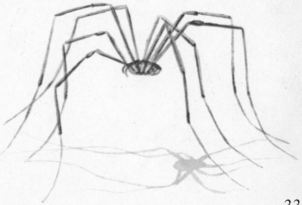

Fish

How many kinds of fish are there?

Scientists have found about 21,000 different kinds of fish. All of them are alike in some ways. They all have bones inside their bodies, and they all live in water. They are all cold-blooded, which means that their body temperature is the same as the water temperature. Almost all fish have fins, which help them swim. And most have scales to protect their bodies.

Yet different kinds of fish look amazingly different. Fish are every color you can imagine—red, green, gray, yellow, purple, orange, blue, and brown. Some have stripes, some have spots, and others have fancy patterns. Many fish are very tiny and many others are very large. Fish vary in shape from short and fat to long and skinny. Some even look like snakes.

How can fish breathe in water?

Fish can breathe in water because of the way their bodies are made. Like all animals, fish need to breathe the gas called oxygen in order to live. Oxygen is in the air and in the water, too. Land animals have lungs, which can take oxygen from air but not from water. Fish don't have lungs. They have gills. Gills can take oxygen from water.

When a fish breathes, it takes water in through its mouth. The water then flows through the gills, which take oxygen out of it. Then the water goes out of the fish's body through little openings on each side of its head.

Water with oxygen in it.

Can any fish live out of water?

Yes, a few fish can live out of water—some for hours, some for days, and some for years! Mudskippers hop around on land and even climb trees. So do climbing perch. Walking catfish can crawl along the ground and breathe air for a few days at a time.

The most amazing fish, though, is the lungfish. In summer, the streams where it lives often dry up. So the lungfish curls up in a ball of mud at the bottom of a stream. It goes to sleep for months or maybe even for years—until the rains come again. While it is sleeping, the lungfish breathes air through a little hole it has made in the mudball. In spite of its name, the lungfish does not have lungs. It has gills, and a special air bladder that it uses to breathe air.

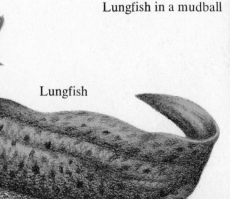

Lungfish in a mudball

Lungfish

35

SHHHH YOU'LL WAKE UP THE FISH

How can fish live in a frozen pond?

If the pond is frozen solid from top to bottom, then fish can *not* live there. Solid ice will not give fish the oxygen they need to keep alive. But usually when we talk about a frozen pond, we mean one with just a covering of ice. This sheet of ice has water below it, and so fish can live in the pond. They usually stay near the bottom of the pond, where the temperature is warmer than near the top.

Do fish sleep?

Most fish do sleep—but with their eyes open! Fish cannot close their eyes, because they have no eyelids. When sleeping, many fish lie on their side or belly at the bottom of the pond, river, or aquarium where they live. The fish that don't sleep take rests. They just stop swimming and stay in one place for a while.

 A grown-up flounder has both eyes on one side of its head!

What do fish eat?

Because so many other water creatures are looking for food, too, most fish eat just about anything they can get. They eat insects, worms, and water animals, including other fish. Some even eat their own babies. There are fish that eat plants, too. But not many eat just plants.

Does a fish feel pain when caught on a hook?

A hooked fish feels very little pain. In order for any animal to feel pain, it must have many nerves in the area that is hurt. The nerves send a message of pain to the animal's brain. A fish has very few nerves around its mouth, where it usually gets hooked. So it cannot feel very much there.

Do fish have voices?

A few do. A fish called the croaker makes a deep, grumpy-sounding "gur-rumph." The sound is made in the fish's belly and is a lot like the noise a bullfrog makes. A fish called the grunting catfish makes a sound, too—but only when you take it out of the water.

School of Fish

What is a school of fish?

A school of fish is not a place where fish learn things. Fish schools are simply groups of fish that stay together. In a school, fish have more protection against hungry enemies. Each school is made up of one kind of fish. You will never find bluefish and herring together in one school. You will never even find baby fish in the same school as adult fish.

How many fish are in a school?

The number of fish in one school can vary from about 25 in a school of tuna to hundreds of millions in a school of sardines.

How fast can fish swim?

The fastest fish is the sailfish, which sometimes swims at more than 60 miles an hour. A few fish can swim between 30 and 45 miles an hour. Most are much slower. A small trout moves along at only 4 miles an hour. But it still swims faster than you do!

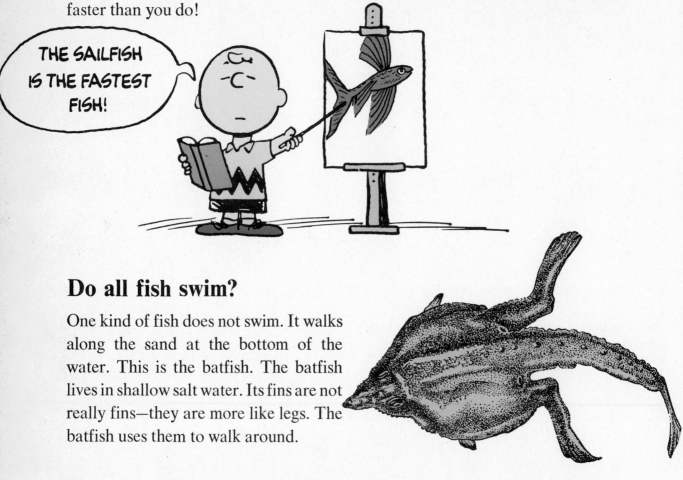

THE SAILFISH IS THE FASTEST FISH!

Do all fish swim?

One kind of fish does not swim. It walks along the sand at the bottom of the water. This is the batfish. The batfish lives in shallow salt water. Its fins are not really fins—they are more like legs. The batfish uses them to walk around.

! The upside-down catfish swims on its back! **!**

STOCKED WITH PYGMY GOBY

What fish is the smallest?

The pygmy goby is the smallest adult fish. It hardly ever grows longer than one-third of an inch, which is only this long: ___ .

What fish is the biggest?

The whale shark is the biggest fish. It can grow up to 59 feet long. And it can weigh up to 15 tons—more than twice as much as an African elephant!

Are sharks dangerous?

Yes, many of them are dangerous. These sharks will eat anything that comes their way, including people. Even a shark's skin is dangerous. It is covered with tiny sharp spines that are like little teeth. You can get hurt just brushing against a shark.

Surprisingly, the biggest shark, the whale shark, is not dangerous to people. It eats only small plants and small water animals.

How did the shark get its name?

The word "shark" comes to us from a Latin word meaning sharp teeth!

Is any fish more dangerous than a shark?

A piranha (pih-RAHN-yuh) may be more dangerous than a shark. Although piranhas are small, they have very sharp teeth. These fish travel in schools of thousands and attack all at once. A school of piranhas can eat all the flesh of a big fish, or even a human, in just a few minutes. Piranhas live only in the Amazon region of South America.

Do flying fish really fly?

No, flying fish do not really fly. They glide through the air. Flying would mean that they flapped their fins the way a bird flaps its wings. But these fish don't move their fins when they are out of the water. They simply spread wide their large fins and sail through the air at great speed. Flying fish glide above the water in order to escape from their enemies, which are mostly dolphins.

When a flying fish wants to glide, it swims very quickly to the top of the water. As its head comes out of the water, the fish gives a powerful flip of its tail. This pushes it into the air. The fish can glide above the sea for two or three hundred yards at a time.

How long can goldfish live?

At least one goldfish is known to have lived 40 years. Most goldfish can live about 17 years. Pet goldfish in aquariums don't usually live so long. They often die young from dirty water or a sudden change in water temperature.

In a large pond, a goldfish can grow to be as long as your arm!

What do baby eels look like?

Baby eels don't look at all like their parents. They look like tiny glass leaves. But as they grow, they change into the long, thin fish we recognize as eels.

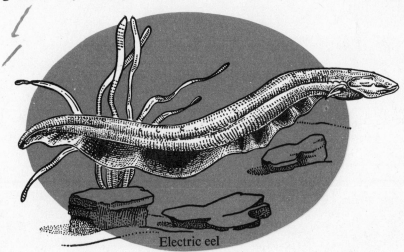

Electric eel

What does an electric eel do with its electricity?

An electric eel uses the electricity in its body to catch food and to scare off enemies. This fish's body is something like a car battery. It makes and stores electricity, which the eel can turn on and off. The shock the eel gives can be strong enough to throw a man across a room. Small water animals are stunned by the shock and can't get away from the hungry eel. Scientists are still trying to find out exactly how this fish makes its electricity.

THE SEA HORSE SWIMS IN AN UPRIGHT POSITION

Is a sea horse a fish?

Yes, a sea horse is a fish, even though it doesn't look much like one. Except for its head, it doesn't look much like a horse either. A sea horse doesn't move the way most fish do. It swims in an upright position, with its head up and its tail pointing down. The one fin on its back moves very quickly and pushes the sea horse along in the water.

Baby sea horses hatch inside a pocket on their **father's** belly!

Are there any sea serpents?

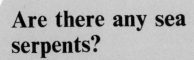

Yes, there are sea serpents, but they are not monsters. They are simply snakes that live in the sea or fish that have snakelike bodies. One of these fish is the oarfish. It grows to be 25 or 30 feet long and has bright red spines sticking out of its head. It looks pretty frightening but is really quite harmless.

What is a mermaid?

The word "mermaid" means sea maiden. Mermaids are supposed to be beautiful sea creatures who are half human and half fish. But mermaids exist only in folk tales. They are not real.

Amphibians

What are amphibians?

Amphibians are animals that live double lives. Most live in the water when they are young. After they have grown up they live on land, although they return to the water to mate and lay eggs. Amphibians are born with gills for breathing in water, just like fish. Later, most of them develop lungs for breathing air. Like fish, amphibians are cold-blooded. Their bodies have the same temperature as the air or water around them.

The amphibians include frogs, toads, salamanders, and caecilians (see-SIL-ee-unz). Caecilians are blind wormlike animals that live underground when grown.

Salamander

Toad

Frog

What is a tadpole?

A tadpole is a baby frog or a baby toad. But it looks more like a fish. Tadpoles have no legs, and they have long tails. They breathe through gills the way fish do. Tadpoles are sometimes called polliwogs.

44

Where does the tadpole's tail go when the tadpole becomes a frog?

As a tadpole changes into a frog, its tail seems to get smaller and smaller. But the tail is not really shrinking. It is changing. It is slowly becoming part of the rest of the tadpole's body. During this time of change, the tadpole grows hind legs, and then a pair of front legs. Its gills change into lungs so it can breathe air. Toad tadpoles change in much the same way as frog tadpoles.

What's the difference between a toad and a frog?

A toad is usually a chubby creature with rough, bumpy skin and no teeth. A frog is thinner, has smooth skin, and usually has teeth. Like all amphibians, frogs and toads are born in the water and return there to mate. But many frogs also spend a large part of their adult lives in the water, while most toads do not. A frog's eggs are often found in big clumps in the water. A toad's eggs are often found in long strings, like beads.

Tree toad

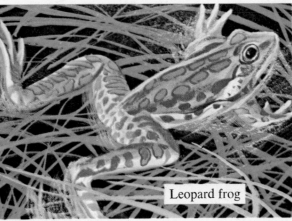

Leopard frog

Can you get warts from a toad?

No, you cannot get warts by touching a toad. That is just superstition. The rough skin of a toad looks as if it is covered with warts, and that is probably why the story got started.

However, the toad is not completely harmless. When a toad is attacked by another animal, it sends out a liquid poison from the bumps on its skin. The poison hurts the attacker's mouth and may keep it from eating the toad, If you catch a toad, and it lets out some of this liquid, be careful not to rub your eyes. The liquid will make them sore. But it will not give you warts.

YOU HAVE TO KISS A LOT OF TOADS BEFORE YOU FIND A PRINCE.

A toad eats about 100 insects every day!

What do frogs eat?

Luckily for us, frogs eat mosquitoes. They also eat flies, moths, beetles, small crayfish, and worms. A frog's mouth is very large. It has two rows of teeth on the upper jaw and none on the lower jaw. A frog has a long sticky tongue attached to the front, not the back, of its mouth. This tongue can be flipped out as quick as a wink to catch insects.

Do people really eat frogs' legs?

Yes, many people enjoy eating frogs' legs. The large hind legs—the jumping legs—are the ones used. They are usually cooked in butter. Most French restaurants have frogs' legs on the menu. Frogs are even raised on frog farms to supply the demand for this unusual dish.

How far can a frog jump?

The longest frog jump on record is 17 feet and 4 inches.

What is the world's largest frog?

The largest frog is the Goliath frog of West Africa. The biggest one ever caught weighed more than seven pounds and was over 32 inches long with its legs spread out.

 The world's smallest frog could fit inside a thimble!

What is the biggest amphibian?

The biggest amphibian is the giant salamander of China and Japan. One found in 1920 was five feet long and weighed almost 100 pounds!

Where do salamanders live?

Adult salamanders are never far from water. They die if they can't keep their skin moist. Some grown salamanders live in ponds and streams. Others live on land, in damp places that are cool and dark. You can find them in shady woods. Often they lie under stones or in hollow logs.

WHAT KIND OF PUPPY NEVER BARKS?

A MUD PUPPY!

What are mud puppies, newts, and efts?

Mud puppies and newts are simply kinds of salamanders. During the time newts are living on land, they are called efts. As efts, they are orange-colored. When they go back to water to mate, they turn green.

Reptiles of Long Ago

What is a reptile?

The word "reptile" means that which crawls. Reptiles are animals that crawl, though some of them prefer to swim. Like fish, reptiles usually have scales on their bodies. But they breathe through lungs, as people do. They are cold-blooded animals. This means that the temperature of their blood changes when the air temperature changes. Snakes, turtles, and lizards are all reptiles. So were dinosaurs.

What are dinosaurs?

Dinosaurs were reptiles that lived a very long time ago—from about 200 million years ago to about 60 million years ago. When dinosaurs first appeared, there were not yet any birds or furry animals on earth. Dinosaurs were of many kinds and many sizes. Some had long waving necks and tails, and some had short, thick bodies. Some lived on land, and others lived in water. Some dinosaurs walked on two legs, and others walked on all four of their legs. There were dinosaurs that ate meat and dinosaurs that ate plants. Many dinosaurs had scales or a tough plate of armor on their bodies. But others had no hard covering at all.

The word "dinosaur" means terrible lizard, and scientists think that some of the dinosaurs *were* terrible and fierce. But others were quiet, peaceful creatures.

The smallest dinosaurs were about the size of chickens, and the biggest were as large as nine or ten elephants!

Were there people living at the same time as dinosaurs?

No. Dinosaurs died out millions of years before the first humans appeared on earth. No person has ever seen a living dinosaur. Cartoons that show cave men riding dinosaurs are just make-believe!

Why did dinosaurs die out?

No one is sure why dinosaurs died out — became "extinct" — but there are a few possible reasons. One is that the climate of the world changed. The warm, wet places where the dinosaurs lived became drier and cooler. The plants that some of the dinosaurs ate could not live in this new climate. When the plants died, the plant-eaters starved to death. When the plant-eating dinosaurs died, so did the meat-eating dinosaurs — since they depended on the plant-eaters for food.

Before dinosaurs became extinct, we know that new kinds of animals appeared on earth. These new animals may have caused the dinosaurs to die out. The animals may have eaten dinosaur eggs. If the eggs were all eaten, there would be no new dinosaurs. Or perhaps the new animals ate the same food as the dinosaurs, and the dinosaurs could no longer find enough to eat.

Another possible reason for the death of the dinosaurs is a world-wide disease that wiped them all out.

Scientists are not satisfied with any one of these reasons. But perhaps all these reasons together explain why dinosaurs became extinct.

How do we know what dinosaurs were like?

Today we are fairly sure what dinosaurs looked like, what they ate, how they walked, and many other things — all because we have found their bones and other remains of their bodies. These remains lay buried in the earth for millions of years and slowly turned to stone. They are called fossils. The word "fossil" means dug up.

The first dinosaur fossils were found in 1818. Many others have been found since. These fossils are mainly dinosaur eggs, bones, and teeth. Scientists can put the bones together into whole skeletons. Then they have a good idea of what dinosaurs actually looked like. By studying fossil teeth, scientists can tell whether a dinosaur ate plants or meat.

Other dinosaur fossils are footprints that have turned to stone. From these, scientists can tell how a dinosaur walked and how heavy it was.

One thing no one knows about dinosaurs is what color they were. Scientists have found prints of dinosaur skin in stone, but they are the color of the stone — not of the dinosaur.

THAT'S A DINOSAUR FOOTPRINT... YOU BLOCKHEADS!

You could easily sit in the footprint of a large dinosaur!

Which were the largest dinosaurs?

Sally is a little confused. "Bronchitis" (bron-KIE-tiss) is a disease that makes people cough. Sally probably meant to say "Brontosaurus" (bron-tuh-SORE-us) which was a very large dinosaur. But it was not the largest. As far as we know, the largest dinosaur was Diplodocus (dih-PLAHD-uh-kuss). It grew to be more than 80 feet long and maybe even as much as 100 feet long. The heaviest dinosaur was Brachiosaurus (bray-key-uh-SORE-us). It probably weighed about as much as 27 taxicabs. Brachiosaurus was so heavy that scientists believe it could hardly move on land. So it spent most of its time in water.

Dinosaur "family tree"

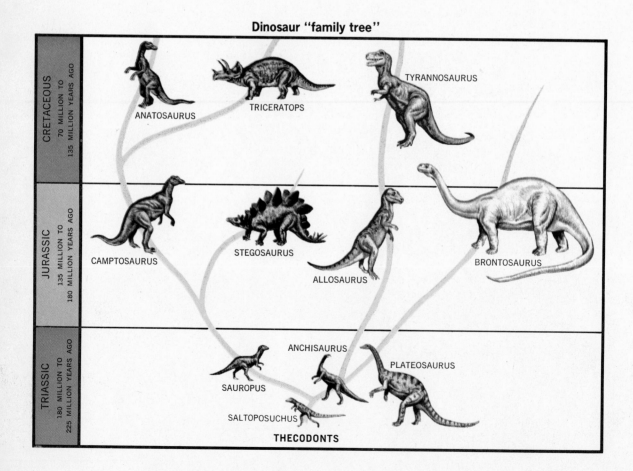

How did dinosaurs get such strange names?

The long, hard-to-pronounce names of dinosaurs all come from Greek words. Greek and Latin are the two languages the earliest scientists used. When modern scientists discover an animal or plant, they still give it a Greek or Latin name. The name is used by scientists all over the world, no matter what language they speak.

When dinosaurs were discovered, scientists gave them Greek names that described what each dinosaur was like. "Tyrannosaurus Rex" means king of the tyrant lizards. "Brontosaurus" means thundering big lizard. This dinosaur was so big that the ground probably shook like thunder when it walked. Stegosaurus (steg-uh-SORE-us) was covered with hard, bony plates and spines. Its name means cover lizard.

Were there any flying dinosaurs?

No. There were no flying dinosaurs, but there were some flying reptiles called Pterodactyls (ter-oh-DACK-tilz). None of these reptiles actually flapped their wings and flew. Instead they all glided through the air — sailed along on the wind. Their wings were made of tough skin stretched between the long front legs and short back legs.

What other reptiles lived in the days of the dinosaurs?

Quite a few water reptiles were around then. One of these was Elasmosaurus (ee-laz-muh-SORE-us). It was probably the closest thing to a sea monster that anyone could imagine. It had a very long neck, and strong legs like flippers for swimming through the water.

Tylosaurus (tie-luh-SORE-us) was a sea reptile that looked something like a modern crocodile. It was a fierce animal with large jaws and very sharp teeth.

Archelon (AR-kuh-lon) was a giant water turtle. The biggest ones weighed 6,000 pounds each and were as long as a large car. Archelon looked very much like any turtle you might see today — except it was much bigger.

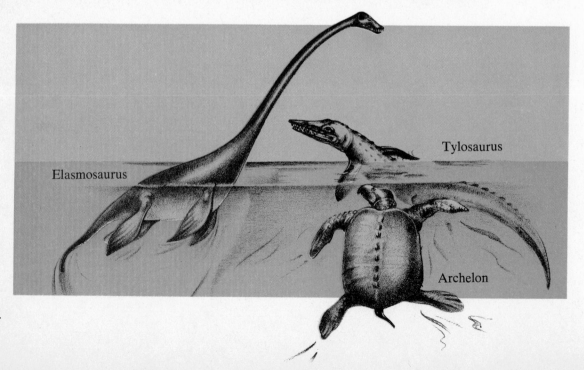

Elasmosaurus

Tylosaurus

Archelon

Reptiles of Today

What kinds of reptiles are living today?

Today there are five kinds of reptiles. These are snakes, lizards, turtles, crocodiles and their relatives, and the tuatara (too-uh-TAH-ruh).

What is the tuatara?

The tuatara is a reptile left over from the days of the dinosaurs. All its closest relatives died a very long time ago. But the tuatara somehow survived in one part of the world — on islands near New Zealand.

The tuatara looks like an odd, big-headed lizard. It does everything slowly. It breathes only once an hour. Its eggs take more than a year to hatch, and a baby takes 20 years to grow up.

Why do reptiles stay underground in winter?

Because reptiles are cold-blooded animals, the temperature of their blood changes with the weather. When the air is warm, their blood is warm, too. When the weather gets cold, the temperature of their blood goes down. The reptiles can get too cold to stay alive. So, to keep from dying, they find a protected place in which to spend the cold days. They may stay in underground holes, in caves, or under rotting tree stumps. Even in these protected places, the reptiles are too cold to move. They lie still until the air warms up. Then they come outside again. Of course, when reptiles live in places that stay warm all year long, they never have to go underground — except to hide.

Which is the biggest reptile living today?

The biggest reptile is the salt-water crocodile. This animal is usually about 13 feet long and weighs about 1,000 pounds. But it sometimes grows even larger.

What is the difference between an alligator and a crocodile?

The easiest way to tell the difference between an alligator and a crocodile is to look at their faces. The crocodile's face is long and pointy. The alligator has a shorter, wider face. When the crocodile's mouth is closed, its teeth still show. But the alligator does not show any teeth when its mouth is closed.

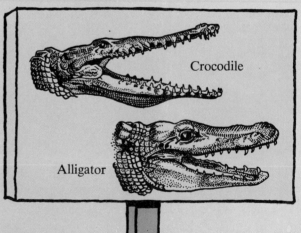

Crocodile

Alligator

Do men really wrestle with alligators?

Yes, they do. You can see these wrestling matches in Florida. Such a match looks very dangerous for the man, but it isn't as dangerous as it seems. An alligator can't bite when its mouth is held shut. So the man just holds the alligator's jaws shut while he wrestles with the animal.

56

Do alligators and crocodiles eat people?

Yes, some of them do eat people. Almost any hungry crocodile or alligator may attack a person who comes close to it. But the African crocodile (found only in Africa) and the salt-water crocodile (found from Southeast Asia to Australia) are the real man-eaters. Hundreds of people are killed by these animals every year. American alligators and crocodiles usually leave people alone.

How slimy are snakes?

Snakes are not at all slimy. In fact, their skins are quite dry, and they feel something like leather. But people may think a snake is slimy when they see one sitting in the sun. When the sun shines on a snake, its skin looks shiny and almost wet.

Why do snakes always stick out their tongues?

Snakes stick out their tongues in order to pick up smells and to feel things. Although many people think a snake's tongue is a stinger, it is perfectly harmless. The snake is simply touching and smelling with it.

57

Why do snakes shed their skins?

As a snake grows, its skin gets too small and tight for it, just as your shoes get too tight when your feet have grown. So the snake grows a new skin and gets rid of — or sheds — the old one. The snake may do this three or four times a year. Because young snakes grow faster than older snakes, the young ones shed their skins more often.

Timber rattlesnake shedding skin

Are snakes useful to us in any way?

Yes. Snakes eat rats, mice, and harmful insects — pests that eat millions of dollars' worth of crops each year and also spread disease. Snakes also eat some animals that are helpful to man, such as insect-eating frogs and birds. But, at least as far as people are concerned, snakes do more good than harm.

How can a thin snake swallow a fat rat?

An amazing thing about snakes is that they swallow their meals whole. Large snakes can swallow whole rats and whole pigs, and sometimes even whole goats!

A snake's jawbones are attached very loosely so that its mouth can stretch very wide. The snake can swallow an animal that is even bigger than its own head. The rest of its body can stretch, too, so the meal can fit inside.

58

A snake swallowing a bird's egg

Do snakes ever eat people?

Although most snakes eat only insects, mice, and other small animals, two kinds of snakes do occasionally feast on a human being. Pythons (which can be found only in Asia and Africa) and anacondas (which can be found only in South America) are the two man-eaters. None of the snakes that live in the United States are big enough to eat people.

GOOD GRIEF. I'M GLAD I LIVE IN THE GOOD OLD U.S.A!

Which is the longest snake?

Some anacondas grow to be more than 20 feet long. The biggest one ever measured was 37½ feet. That's about as long as seven bicycles lined up in a row.

Are fangs teeth?

Yes, a snake's fangs are a special kind of teeth. All snakes have teeth, but only poisonous snakes have fangs. Fangs are hollow teeth with a tiny hole at the bottom. When a fanged snake bites an animal, a poison called venom is forced through the fangs into the victim. A poisonous snake bites small animals in order to kill them for food. A snake bites people and other large animals only if it is scared and wants to protect itself.

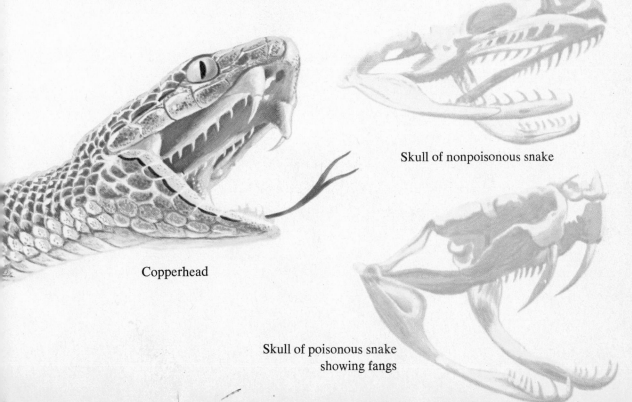

Copperhead

Skull of nonpoisonous snake

Skull of poisonous snake
showing fangs

59

How many snakes are poisonous?

Actually, only 200 of the 2,400 known kinds of snakes are poisonous.

COPPERHEAD!
COPPERHEAD!!
COPPERHEAD!!!

Do any poisonous snakes live in the United States?

Yes, four kinds of poisonous snakes live in the United States. These are the rattlesnake, the copperhead, the water moccasin, and the coral snake. Of these four, the coral snake has the strongest venom. Fortunately, the coral snake is small and scarcely ever bites anyone. The other three kinds of poisonous snakes have venom that takes a long time to kill a person. The victim has time to go to a doctor and get an anti-venom shot.

Sonora Mountain king snakes look almost exactly like poisonous coral snakes. But they are so friendly and harmless that people keep them as pets!

Coral Snake

How do rattlesnakes rattle?

At the end of a rattlesnake's tail are a few hard rings, made of a material something like your fingernails. When the rattlesnake is excited, it usually shakes its tail. The hard rings hit against each other, making a rattling noise.

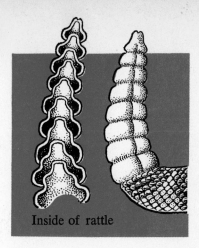
Inside of rattle

Can snakes be charmed?

No. In India, men called snake charmers play music for cobra snakes, and the cobras seem to dance to it. But they are not really dancing. The snakes cannot even hear the music—they are completely deaf! But the snakes can feel vibrations in the ground. A snake charmer taps his foot as he plays and sways in time to the music. A cobra feels the tapping, gets excited, and rears up ready to strike him. When a cobra is ready to strike, it watches its victim carefully and follows the victim's movements. And that's just what a cobra does with a snake charmer.

The snake charmer is taking a big chance when he excites a cobra. Cobras have a deadly venom and strike at people often. But somehow the snake charmer knows how to keep an excited cobra from actually striking. He really must know his business! Some snake charmers remove the cobras' fangs to be on the safe side.

ALLEGRO!!

61

THAT'S TERRIBLE..

The matamata turtle has wormy-looking bumps on its neck that fish try to eat. But instead, the matamata eats the fish!

How long can a turtle live?

No one is sure how long turtles live, but some can probably live for a very long time—100 or maybe even 150 years.

Spotted turtle

Can you tell the age of a turtle by its shell?

By looking at its shell, you can tell the age of a young turtle, but not of an old turtle. The top of a turtle's shell is divided into sections. These are called shields. On each shield are little circles. In a young turtle, each circle stands for a year's growth. For example, a two-year-old turtle has two circles on each shield. After five or ten years, however, you can no longer find out the turtle's age by the circles. They have either become too crowded together or have begun to wear off.

Wood-turtle shell showing shields

Can a turtle crawl out of its shell?

No, a turtle cannot crawl out of its shell. The shell is attached to some of the turtle's bones.

62

Common pond turtle

Where do turtles live?

Some turtles live in rivers, lakes, or ponds but often come out on land. These are sometimes called terrapins. Other turtles—ones with flippers—spend most of their life swimming in the ocean. There are also large turtles that always live on land. These have fat legs that look somewhat like an elephant's. People sometimes call these turtles tortoises (TORE-tus-uz).

Which is the largest turtle?

The largest turtle is the leatherback. It is a sea turtle that usually weighs between 600 and 800 pounds. The biggest one ever caught weighed nearly 2,000 pounds and was almost eight feet long.

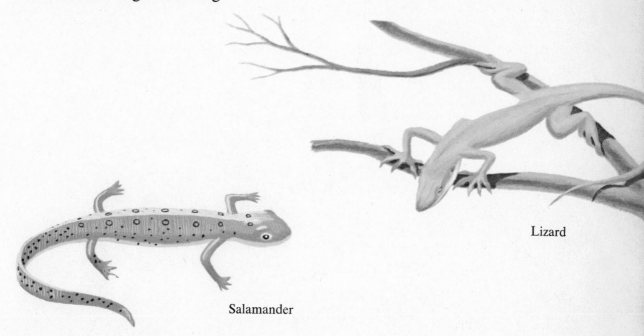

Lizard

Salamander

What is the difference between a lizard and a salamander?

Some lizards look very much like salamanders. However, the two animals are quite different. Salamanders are amphibians. Most amphibians begin their life in water, breathing through gills like fish. Only after they have grown up are they able to live on land. Lizards, which are reptiles, are born with lungs. They always live on land.

Lizards have scales covering their bodies. Salamanders have smooth, moist skins without scales. Lizards love the sun, while salamanders stay away from it.

Can lizards grow new tails?

Some lizards can. The gecko, the glass snake, and the skink are three of the lizards that grow new tails. If an enemy catches one of them by the tail, the lizard can drop the tail and run away. The lizard then grows a new tail. If only a piece of its tail is broken off, the lizard will sometimes grow back the missing piece and grow a whole new tail as well. So if you ever see a lizard with two tails, you'll know how it got them.

Are any lizards poisonous?

Only two out of about 3,000 known kinds of lizards are poisonous. One of these is the Mexican beaded lizard. The other is its cousin, the Gila (HEE-luh) monster. The Gila monster lives in Mexico and in the southwestern United States. People can die from the bites of these two lizards, but seldom do. The lizards don't usually put enough poison into people to kill them.

Can lizards change their color?

Some lizards can. These include the anole, sometimes called the American chameleon (kuh-MEE-lee-un), and the true chameleons. They can turn different shades of brown and green. Their color depends on the amount of light hitting them, the temperature of the air, and whether they are calm or scared.

A chameleon often turns the same color as its background. A chameleon on a log may be brown, and one on leaves may be green. Enemies have a hard time spotting it. And if a chameleon is partly in the sun and partly in the shade, an enemy can get really confused—because the chameleon will be two different colors at once!

GILA
CHAMELEON

Is the horned toad a reptile?

Yes. In spite of its name, the horned toad is not a toad at all. It is a kind of lizard that lives in the desert.

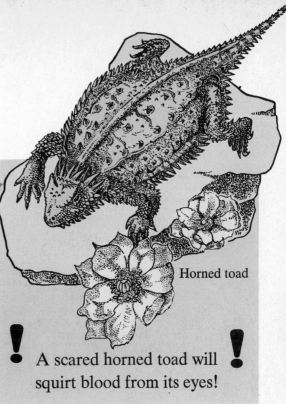

Horned toad

A scared horned toad will squirt blood from its eyes!

Do dragons really exist?

Dragons like the ones in storybooks do not exist. Long ago, people believed that there were great winged reptiles that breathed out fire. People in Europe believed that these dragons were evil. The Chinese, on the other hand, believed that these dragons were gods.

Today there do exist huge reptiles called Komodo dragons. They are the largest lizards alive. These dragons can grow to be ten feet long and weigh 300 pounds. They look like storybook dragons without wings. But they do not breathe fire, and they are not evil. Neither are they gods. They are simply huge animals that get hungry and have to eat. Any living creature around a hungry Komodo dragon had better watch out!

Birds

What was the world's very first bird?

The first bird was Archaeopteryx (ar-kee-OP-ter-ix). It lived about 140 million years ago. This bird was very much like a reptile. In fact, its ancestors *were* reptiles. Like a reptile, Archaeopteryx had teeth and a long, bony tail. But Archaeopteryx had feathers instead of scales. For this reason scientists call it a bird. The wings of Archaeopteryx were like a modern bird's wings—with bones inside and feathers outside. But Archaeopteryx was not able to fly well. It couldn't flap its wings very hard. It probably used them more for gliding—sailing through the air.

Archaeopteryx

What is a bird?

Any animal that has feathers is a bird. All birds have two wings and two legs. Except for bats, they are the only living animals with bones that can fly. Modern birds have no teeth. But they have a hard mouth part, called a bill or beak, which helps them catch and eat their food. All birds lay eggs, and most birds build nests for the eggs to hatch in. Birds—like people—are "warm-blooded." Their body temperature stays about the same no matter how hot or cold the air is.

Hummingbird

66

How many different birds are there?

About 9,000 kinds of birds live on the earth today. Birds can be found almost everywhere except the North and South poles.

Why do birds have feathers?

Feathers help a bird to keep warm. In cold weather, a bird fluffs up its feathers and traps a layer of warm air under them. The fluffed feathers act as a blanket by holding in body heat. In warmer weather a bird squeezes its feathers against its body to let body heat escape.

Feathers also help a bird to fly. In flight, a bird uses its outer wing feathers to move forward in the air. Wing feathers and tail feathers are both used for balancing, steering, and braking.

Why do some male birds have brighter colors than females?

Bright colors help a male bird to attract a mate. His colors are brightest during the mating season. He flies or parades in front of a female, showing off his pretty feathers. He may also sing or dance to get her attention.

Scarlet tanagers

WOODSTOCK'S NEST →

NEXT NINE EXITS

How do birds learn to build nests?

Birds don't learn to build nests. Nest-building is an instinct. Each kind of bird is born knowing how to build its own kind of nest. Many birds make a cup-shaped nest out of twigs and grass. Cardinals and thrushes make this kind of nest. Some swallows make their nests out of mud balls, which they attach to cliffs or the eaves of buildings. Some birds, such as titmice, make their nests in a hole in a tree or rock. They line the bottom of the hole with grass, feathers, fur, and moss. Certain weaverbirds make complicated "apartment-house" nests out of stems. These nests may be ten feet high and hold 100 or more birds.

Swainson's thrushes

Cliff swallow

Do all bird eggs look like chicken eggs?

Most eggs are shaped the same as chicken eggs, but they have different sizes and colors. Large birds lay large eggs, and small birds lay small eggs. The colors of eggs vary from one kind of bird to another. The eggs often blend in with the colors around the nest so an enemy can't spot them easily. Eggs may be light blue, brown, white, gray, or green. A few are red or pinkish orange. Some eggs are spotted or speckled.

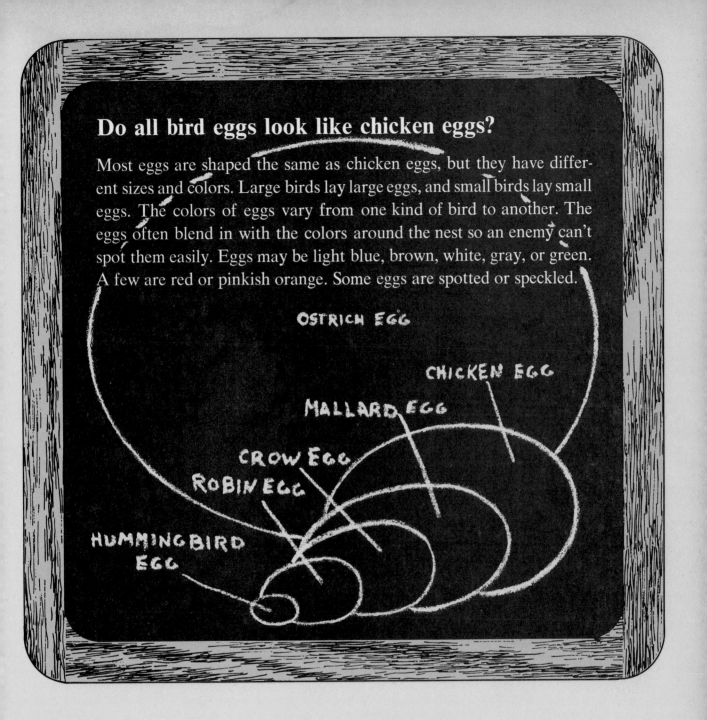

OSTRICH EGG

CHICKEN EGG

MALLARD EGG

CROW EGG

ROBIN EGG

HUMMINGBIRD EGG

Which bird lays the smallest egg?

A hummingbird—which is the smallest bird—lays the smallest egg. Its egg is only about half an inch long.

Which bird lays the biggest egg?

The ostrich—which is the biggest bird—lays the biggest egg. This egg can be as long as eight inches and can weigh up to four pounds.
If a 250-pound animal sat down on an ostrich egg, the egg would not break!

Why do birds sit on their eggs?

Birds sit on their eggs to keep them warm. When an egg is kept warm, the baby bird inside can grow.

Do all birds eat worms?

No. Different kinds of birds eat different kinds of food. Usually birds have favorite foods, but will eat some other things, too. Many birds like worms and insects best. Birds that live near water often eat fish or shellfish. Owls, hawks, and eagles eat meat — mice, rabbits, smaller birds, snakes, and other animals. Many small birds, such as sparrows, live on seeds. Some birds eat mostly fruit and berries. Hummingbirds like to drink the sweet liquid called nectar that is found in flowers.

Why do woodpeckers peck at trees?

Woodpeckers peck at trees to get food. They eat insects that live in the trees, just under the bark. Most woodpeckers also peck out nesting holes in trees.

Great black-backed gull

Herring gull

Why can birds fly?

A bird's body is specially built for flying. It is very light. There are pockets of air in it, and most of the bones are hollow. So a bird doesn't have to lift much weight into the air. A bird has very strong muscles for flapping its wings. And the wings have just the right shape for flying. The inner part of a bird's wing is like the wing of an airplane. It lifts the bird up in the air. The outer part of the wing acts as a propeller. Its long feathers pull on the air and move the bird forward.

GOOD GRIEF, WOODSTOCK'S IN LOVE AGAIN

Some birds will fly upside down to attract a mate!

Can all birds fly?

No, a few birds cannot fly, but most of them are very fast runners or swimmers. The ostrich, the cassowary (KASS-uh-wer-ee), the rhea (REE-uh), the emu (EE-myu), and the kiwi (KEE-wee) are all non-fliers. They have wings, but their flying muscles are not strong enough to be useful. Penguins also can't fly. They have wings like flippers, which they use to swim and dive powerfully. Chickens cannot fly very well, but they can flutter around a bit.

Adelie penguin

Blue Throated
Hummingbird

Ruby Topaz
Hummingbird

How can a hummingbird stand still in the air?

A hummingbird can stand still, or "hover," in the air because it can beat its wings very fast—from 55 to 90 times in one second! Its wings move so fast that they look like a blur. A hummingbird hovers in front of flowers when it drinks nectar from them.

Why do birds sing?

Bird songs are not just pretty music. Birds usually sing to tell other birds of their kind to keep away from their nesting area. Often birds sing to attract a mate. And sometimes they seem to sing just for the fun of it.

Nightingale

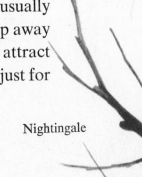

Do all birds sing?

No. Female birds rarely sing, and only about half the males have songs. But nearly all birds give calls. Calls are short, simple sounds. The "whoo-whoo" of an owl is a call. So is the "cluck-cluck" of a hen.

Calls are often used to express alarm and warn other birds of danger. Birds "talk" to their babies with calls. Baby birds use calls to say they are hungry. Non-singing males have special calls that take the place of songs.

A small number of adult birds make no sounds at all. But these birds do make a lot of noise when they are young.

Where do birds go in the winter?

Before winter comes, many birds that live in the north fly south where the weather is warmer. In the spring, they fly north again. We say that those birds "migrate." No one is sure why birds began migrating, but the need for food was probably the main reason. In cold places there are few insects, flowers, fruits, and seeds around for birds to eat. Ponds and streams are frozen over, so fishing birds cannot get food either. In warm places, food of all kinds is available. ——

Every year Arctic terns fly 11,000 miles south to Antarctica and 11,000 miles back home again. They fly 22,000 miles each year!

BIRDS OF A FEATHER MAY MIGRATE TOGETHER BUT NOT WOODSTOCK. HE GETS TOO HOMESICK.

How do birds know when to fly south?

No one is sure of the exact answer to this question. We do know that in the fall the weather gets cooler, and the days get shorter. Somehow these changes affect a bird's body so that the bird knows it's time to migrate. Scientists are still trying to find out exactly what happens inside birds at migration time.

Does an ostrich really stick its head in the sand to hide from an enemy?

No, an ostrich isn't that stupid. What this tall bird does is fall down flat when it sees danger in the distance. An enemy may not spot the ostrich in this position, or it may think the ostrich is just a bush. As soon as danger comes near, however, the ostrich will take off and run. Although an ostrich cannot fly, it can run as fast as 40 miles an hour.

Are owls really wise?

Owls are no wiser than many other birds. In fact, some birds are smarter. But owls have large staring eyes, which make them look as if they are thinking very hard. That's probably why people started calling them wise.

!!

An owl turns its whole head upside down in order to see above it!

Which is the most dangerous bird?

The cassowary is the most dangerous bird in the world. It has a sharp claw on each foot and can kick very, very hard. One kick can cripple or kill a grown person.

Brown creeper

How do birds protect themselves?

Birds protect themselves by always listening and watching for danger. At the smallest sign of it, they will fly away. That's why it is almost impossible to get very close to a wild bird. Birds that cannot fly are often able to swim fast, or run quickly and kick, too. Some birds—such as owls—make themselves look bigger and more dangerous by fluffing out their feathers. Other birds will hiss at enemies and scare them away.

Another important protection for many birds is their color. Their feathers often have colors and patterns that match the things around their nest. Some birds are streaked with colors that imitate leaves, bark, or grass. Some birds, such as the ptarmigan (TAR-muh-gun), change colors with the seasons. In the winter the ptarmigan is white to match the snow. In the summer it is mostly brown to match the ground.

Why have some birds become extinct?

Some kinds of birds have become extinct because people have killed all of them. In the past, hunters killed birds for their colored feathers, their oil, or their meat. Today some farmers are killing large birds that sometimes eat small farm animals. Certain eagles and hawks may become extinct for this reason.

People also kill birds without meaning to. When people cut down forests and fill in swamps to build houses and factories, they destroy the homes and the food of birds. If the birds have nowhere else to go and nothing to eat, they die out.

Pollution may soon cause some birds to become extinct. Birds that eat fish from polluted water get poison in their bodies. Then they can't lay healthy eggs. New birds aren't born.

The dodo, the passenger pigeon, the great auk, and the Carolina parakeet are some of the birds that have become extinct. Other birds have nearly died out. But they have been saved because people who care have protected them.

Americans have shot and killed hundreds of thousands of bald eagles. Yet the bald eagle is our national bird!

How do people protect birds?

People protect birds by passing laws to control hunting and pollution, by setting up special parks called bird sanctuaries (SANK-choo-er-eez) where all birds are safe from hunters, and by teaching other people to care about birds rather than kill them.

Mammals of Long Ago

What are mammals?

Mammals are animals that drink milk from their mother's body when they are babies. No other animals do this. Most baby mammals grow inside their mother's belly before they are born. Most other animals grow inside eggs that their mother lays.

All mammals are warm-blooded. This means that their body temperature always stays about the same. And they are the only animals that have hair or fur. (Some insects are fuzzy, but they don't have real hair.) Most mammals have four legs, or two arms and two legs.

Dogs are mammals. So are cats, giraffes, bats, cows, horses, rats, monkeys, and dolphins. And you are a mammal, too.

THAT'S RIGHT. YOU'RE A MAMMAL AND SO ARE CATS AND RATS AND MONKEYS.

I HATE THOSE COMPARISONS!

When did the first mammals appear?

The first mammals appeared about 180 million years ago. They probably looked a lot like shrews or rats, having long, pointed snouts and long tails. There were few kinds of mammals on earth at first, but there were great numbers of dinosaurs. As many of the huge reptiles began to die out, mammals became the most common land animals. This change began about 65 million years ago. At that time, many new kinds of mammals appeared on earth.

78

What were some of these new kinds of mammals?

The ancestor of the horse—the eohippus (ee-o-HIP-us)—was one. This animal was about the size of a small dog. It had three toes on each hind foot and four toes on each front foot. Over millions of years, the horse grew bigger and bigger, until it got to be the size it is now. And over the years it lost some toes, and so now it has only one on each foot.

Eohippus

About 25 million years ago, the first doglike and catlike animals appeared. Some of the cats developed into large, fierce animals. One was the saber-toothed tiger. It was about the size of a modern tiger, but two of its front teeth were very long—about eight inches!—and very sharp. Even the largest animals were probably scared of it.

One of these large animals was the rhinoceros. It too started out small. But as millions of years passed, it became larger and larger. Huge groups of rhinos moved north to cold lands and grew thick coats of hair. These rhinos were called the "woolly" rhinos.

Saber-toothed tiger

There were also woolly mammoths. These appeared about two million years ago and became extinct only about ten thousand years ago. Mammoths were related to elephants. They were very large and had long, thick hair. Scientists know exactly how they looked, because whole mammoths have been found frozen in ice.

Millions of years ago there were also many odd-looking beasts. They lived for hundreds of thousands of years and then died out. One was Glyptodont (GLIP-toe-dahnt). It was very much like a modern armadillo, but a lot larger. Glyptodont was about 15 feet long and had a tough shell around its body—much like a turtle's. At the end of its tail were spikes. Glyptodont probably used its tail as a club and swung it at enemies.

Woolly mammoth

Ancient Glyptodont

79

! The dog family has been on earth for about 15 million years! !

How do we know about early mammals?

We know about them because people have found stone fossils of their bones and teeth in the earth. And people have found real bones and teeth in large pits of tar in La Brea, California. About one million years ago, thousands of animals sank into these tar pits and died. The tar hardened and kept their bones almost perfectly. The bones were very easy to dig out and to study. Saber-toothed tigers, mammoths, vultures, snakes, camels, and ground sloths were some of the animals found in the La Brea tar pits.

Many mammals have also been found frozen in the ice in the far north. Just the way a freezer keeps food from spoiling, the frozen ice kept whole animals from rotting away for hundreds of thousands of years. Many woolly mammoths and woolly rhinos have been found in ice.

An excellent record of animals that lived about 35,000 years ago was left by early people. These people lived in caves and painted pictures of animals on the cave walls.

Which was the biggest land mammal ever to live?

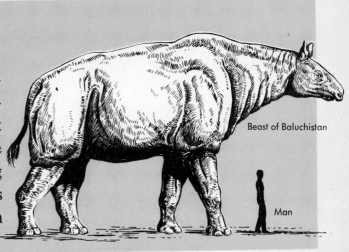

Beast of Baluchistan

Man

The beast of Baluchistan (buh-loo-chih-STAN). This huge animal looked something like an overgrown rhinoceros. It died out about 20 million years ago. The beast could grow as large as 37 feet long and 25 feet tall. It weighed as much as 22 tons. One of its legs alone was much larger than a grown man!

When did people appear on earth?

According to scientists, the first real people appeared on earth about two and a half million years ago.

What did the first people look like?

Scientists think they probably had thick hairy bodies, no chins, short necks, and long arms. Enough bones have been found to make us believe that these people stood about five feet tall. But they did not stand completely straight. Instead, they walked with their heads bent forward. These people had bigger brains than other animals, and they were smarter. They made the first stone tools and figured out how to build a fire.

KIND OF SHAKES YOU UP, DOESN'T IT?

SIR?

Dinosaurs were on earth about 140 million years.
People have been on earth only about 2½ million years!

Mammals of Today

Why is a whale called a mammal?

A whale lives in water, and has a fishlike shape and no legs. But a whale is not a fish. It is a mammal, and it acts like one. A whale—like other mammals—grows inside its mother, is born alive, drinks milk from its mother's body, breathes air through lungs, is warm-blooded, and has some hair but no scales. A fish, on the other hand, usually hatches from an egg, does not drink milk, breathes underwater through gills, is cold-blooded, and usually has scales.

LAUGH IF YOU WISH, MY FINE-FINNED-FRIENDS. IT'S CALLED A DOG PADDLE.

Is there any mammal that doesn't grow hair?

No. Every mammal has some hair at some time in its life. The dolphin, a relative of the whale, has no hair when it is grown up. But it is born with a few bristles of hair around its snout. The armadillo has a scaly shell like some reptiles. But it also has hair on the underside of its body. The pangolin (pang-GO-lin) is covered with scales, but they are made of hairs that are stuck together. Porcupines and hedgehogs have sharp "needles" coming out of their bodies. These needles are really a special kind of hair called quills.

Can porcupines shoot their quills?

No, they can't. But their quills are sometimes found stuck in other animals. That's probably how the "shooting" story got started. Actually, porcupine quills get stuck in an animal when the porcupine touches it. The quills come off the porcupine very easily. Its tail is particularly full of loose quills. When another animal attacks, the porcupine swings its tail at the enemy. Quills are driven deep into the enemy's flesh. The enemy runs off in pain. Animals that attack porcupines learn their lesson quickly and don't bother them again.

Why do beavers build dams?

Beavers build dams in the shallow water of streams in order to make the water deeper. A beaver dam is a wall that keeps water from flowing past it. The water builds up behind the dam and gets deep. The beavers then build their home in the deep water, where enemies can't easily reach them.

How do beavers build dams?

Beavers have four very sharp front teeth. With these teeth, they cut down trees and then cut the trees into pieces. The cut logs and branches are used to make their dams.

A family of beavers usually work together to build a dam. They make a base of logs across a narrow part of a stream. They weigh it down with rocks and mud. On top of this heap, they pile more and more logs and branches. They fill in the holes with mud, which they carry to the dam in their front paws as they swim through the water. A finished dam is a wall about three or four feet high.

83

Beaver

! One group of beavers built a dam more than 2,000 feet long. That's longer than the Brooklyn Bridge in New York City! !

Can groundhogs predict weather?

No, they can't. Groundhogs, also known as woodchucks, hibernate all winter in a hole in the ground. The story goes that on February 2—Groundhog Day—the groundhog comes up out of its hole. If the day is cloudy and the groundhog can't see its shadow, the cold days of winter are over. If the groundhog sees its shadow, the animal returns to its hole. Then we are supposed to have six more weeks of cold weather.

This story is fun, but there is no truth to it. Groundhogs stay in their holes until the weather warms up enough for them to come out. This may happen much later than February 2, or even earlier. Once outside, groundhogs don't look for shadows. They just go about their business—which is *not* predicting the weather!

What does "playing possum" mean?

Charlie Brown knows what he's talking about. The expression "playing possum" comes from a habit of an animal called the possum, or opossum. It falls over limp, as if it were dead, whenever danger is near. This act protects the opossum. Most meat-eating animals like to kill their own meals. They are not interested in an animal that lies still and already seems to be dead.

People used to think that the opossum purposely played a trick on its enemies by pretending to be dead. But now we know that the possum passes out when danger is near. It is not playing at all.

Why do skunks give off a bad smell?

Skunks give off a bad smell to protect themselves from enemies. When a skunk is angry or frightened, it shoots an oily spray into the air. This bad-smelling spray comes from two openings near the skunk's tail. If the spray hits the face of an animal, it burns and stings. It also tastes terrible. But the smell alone is enough to chase away any enemy.

When the spotted skunk gets ready to spray, it stands on its front legs with its back ones in the air!

Do cats really have nine lives?

No, cats don't have nine lives. But they seem to because they often live through dangers that might kill another kind of animal. For example, cats can walk on a very narrow ledge without falling off. They have a very good sense of balance. If they do fall or jump from a fairly high place, they almost always land on their feet — lightly and unharmed. Cats can also escape easily from an enemy because they can move quickly.

SO YOU FINALLY DID IT. YOU GOT INTO A FIGHT WITH THE CAT NEXT DOOR.

IT WAS A MASSACRE. NINE LIVES AGAINST ONE!

Why do a cat's eyes shine at night?

A cat's eyes shine because they reflect light. Even in the darkest night, there is usually some stray light from a street lamp or the headlights of a car. A cat's eyes reflect this light because they have a special coating on them. The coating helps the cat see in the dark, and also makes the cat's eyes shine.

House cats are not the only cats with eyes that reflect light. Jaguars, lions, tigers, cougars, leopards, and all other cats have eyes that shine at night.

What is the world's fastest mammal?

The fastest mammal is a wild cat called the cheetah. It can run at more than 60 miles an hour, and sometimes as fast as 70 miles an hour. But the cheetah can keep up this speed for only a short distance. Then it slows down.

SPEED LIMIT 55

WILD CATS! I HOPE THEY GET A TICKET!

Cheetahs

Cougar, puma, panther, painter, mountain lion, catamount, American lion, and Indian devil are all names for the same kind of wild cat!

Why does a dog wag its tail?

Tail wagging is one of the ways that a dog "talks." You know that a dog is feeling happy when it wags its tail at you. Dogs also use tail wags to give special messages to other dogs. One kind of wag means, "Hello. Glad to see you." Another means, "I'm the boss around here." And a third means "Okay, you're the boss."

Why do dogs pant?

Dogs pant to cool off when they are feeling hot. People cool off by sweating, but dogs don't sweat very much. Instead, they breathe hard, with their tongues hanging out. This brings air into their bodies. The air cools their insides.

Why do dogs turn in circles before they lie down?

The ancestors of dogs were wild animals that lived outside. They turned around and around in circles to flatten grass and make a comfortable bed. Modern house dogs are still born with the instinct to make beds for themselves in this way —even though they no longer need this instinct. But wild dogs do need it. They still make their beds in grass by turning in circles.

Why do dogs gobble their food?

Charlie Brown is absolutely right. When dogs were wild, they didn't have owners to feed them. They had to hunt for their food. They would hunt in groups called packs. After they had killed an animal, each dog would try to get as much of the food as it could. But the wild dogs were not just trying to beat each other. If they didn't eat the food quickly, a larger animal might come along and take it away. Dogs today are still born with the instinct to gobble.

Earth's first space traveler was a dog!

Red Wolves

Do wolves ever attack people?

The wolves in the United States and Canada don't attack people. In fact, they stay as far away from people as possible. All the stories of wolf attacks probably grew up around Russian wolves. These wolves seem to be a more dangerous kind than the others. Even so, scientists don't believe most of the stories.

Why does a cow keep chewing when she isn't eating?

A cow has a special stomach with four parts. When she eats some grass, she chews it just enough to make it wet. Then it goes into the first part of her stomach, where it becomes softer. From there it goes into the second part, where it is made into little balls called "cuds." Later, while the cow is resting, she brings up each cud one at a time and chews it well. When she swallows it, the food goes into the third part of her stomach. There the water is squeezed out of it. Finally, the food goes to the fourth part of the cow's stomach and is broken down into very tiny pieces. Then the cow's body can take what it needs from the food to live and grow.

Do bulls really attack when they see red?

No, they don't. Bull fighters always wave a red cape in front of a bull. But the color red is not what makes the bull charge. In fact, the bull is color-blind. He cannot see the color red. Instead, the bull sees the movements of the cape and gets excited.

Bactrian Camel

Arabian Camel
or Dromedary

Why do camels have humps?

Camels live in the desert. They sometimes have to go for a long time without any food. That's when their humps become useful. The humps are made of fat. The camel can get its energy from the fat if it has no food. When the camel has not eaten for a few days, its humps get smaller. They get big again after the camel has filled itself up with food.

Is a pony a baby horse?

No, a baby horse is called a foal. A pony is a kind of horse that just happens to be small. When fully grown, it is between 32 and 58 inches tall. It weighs less than 800 pounds. That doesn't seem very small until you compare a pony to other horses. A large workhorse can weigh more than 2,000 pounds!

Shetland Pony

Workhorse

Why does a zebra have stripes?

A zebra's stripes help this animal to hide from enemies. When you see a zebra in the zoo, its stripes make it stand out clearly. But normally the zebra lives in places where there is very tall grass. There, the zebra's stripes blend in with the shadows of the blades of grass.

Which mammal is most like a human?

The chimpanzee. It is built a lot like us. It often walks on two feet the way we do. And, like us, it has no tail. However, the chimp is much smaller than a person. It has longer arms, shorter legs and a more hairy body.

The chimpanzee is probably the smartest animal next to man. A chimp can be taught to do almost everything a three-year-old child can do. One chimpanzee learned to say and understand a few English words. Others have learned to use the sign language of deaf and of mute people. Chimps have their own language, too. They have at least 20 different sounds that they use to "talk" to each other. Like humans, chimps show many different emotions in their faces. Sadly for the chimps, they also get human diseases such as cancer and tuberculosis.

What good is the giraffe's long neck?

With its long neck and long legs, the giraffe is the tallest animal in the world. Its head may be 19 feet above the ground. The giraffe's great height helps it in two ways. First, the giraffe can easily see a great distance over the flat open land where it lives. If a hungry lion is anywhere near, the giraffe will spot it soon enough to run away. Second, the giraffe can eat the leaves high up on trees. Other animals cannot reach these leaves. So the giraffe doesn't have to worry about their eating its food.

How does an elephant use its trunk?

A trunk is used as a nose, hand, and arm by an elephant. The elephant uses its trunk to smell, to feel along the ground, and to pick up objects. At the tip of its trunk it has either one or two "fingers" which can pick up something as small as a peanut. With its whole trunk, it can lift something as large as a tree.

An elephant uses its trunk to show affection. A mother pets her baby with her trunk. Both males and females pet each other with their trunks during mating season.

An elephant can also take up water with its trunk. It drinks by spraying the water into its mouth. Sometimes it sprays water all over its back. This shower keeps the elephant cool and clean.

SUDDENLY I HAVE THIS FEELING THAT I'M NOT ALONE!

GAME PRESERVE
OPEN TO THE PUBLIC

Why does a kangaroo have a pouch?

A female kangaroo has a pouch so that her baby will have a place to live. When the kangaroo is born, it is only about an inch long — skinny, hairless, and very helpless. It is not yet ready to live in the outside world. So it crawls across its mother's body and into her pouch. There it can keep warm and safe and drink its mother's milk.

The baby kangaroo stays completely inside its mother's pouch about six months. Then it begins to stick its head out to eat leaves from low branches. When the baby kangaroo gets big enough to walk around, its mother still keeps an eye on it. She pulls it back into the pouch when danger is near.

WALTZING MATILDA

MELBOURNE →

If you annoy a llama, it will spit in your face!

Spiny Anteater

Do any mammals lay eggs?

Yes, two kinds of mammals lay eggs. One is the platypus (PLAT-ih-pus), or duckbill, and the other is the spiny anteater. They are both called mammals because they have some kind of hair and the mothers feed their babies milk.

The female platypus lays from one to three eggs inside a hole in the ground. She keeps them warm with her tail until they hatch. Then she feeds the babies milk that comes out of the skin on her belly. Her way of feeding milk is different from that of most female mammals, whose milk comes out of special nipples on the chest or belly.

The female spiny anteater lays only one egg. She keeps it in a pouch that is something like a kangaroo's pouch. After it hatches, the baby stays in the pouch to drink milk that—like the platypus's milk—comes out of its mother's skin.

Platypus

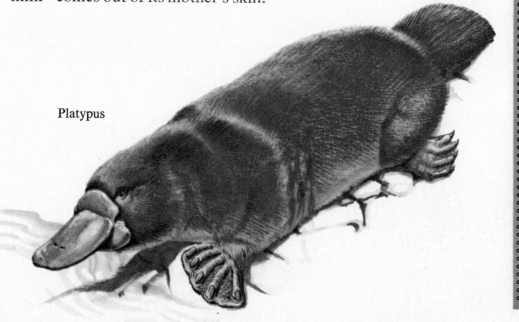

Mastiff Bat

Pipistrelle Bat

Do any mammals fly?

Only one kind of mammal can fly—and that is the bat. Like birds, bats have wings that they can flap.

"Flying" squirrels and "flying" lemurs can't really fly—they glide. Instead of wings, these mammals have a piece of furry skin stretched between each front and back leg. This skin acts as a parachute when the animals leap from tree to tree.

Vampire

Natterer's Bat

How blind are bats?

Bats are not at all blind. They can see. In fact, some see very well. However, bats come out mostly at night and many of them have a hard time seeing in the dark. At night, these bats use their ears in place of eyes. The bats give out little clicking sounds. They can tell by the echo from each sound how near or far away an object is.

Mexican
Freetailed Bat

Hoary Bat

Most bats sleep hanging upside down! **!!**

You and How You Grow

What are you made of?

Yes, you are made of cells. Every part of you—your bones, your muscles, your skin, your blood, your nerves, your teeth, your hair—is made of cells. These cells are so tiny that you can see them only under a microscope. Your whole body is made up of trillions and trillions of them.

What do cells look like?

This is a picture of one tiny cell as it looks under a microscope.

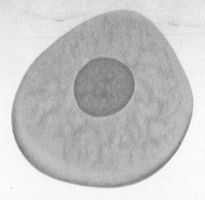

Not all cells look exactly like this one. Different parts of your body are made up of different kinds of cells.

Each kind of cell does a special job that no other kind of cell can do. For example, muscle cells can tighten and relax to make your body move. One kind of blood cell can kill harmful germs. Nerve cells can send messages to your brain and other parts of your body.

Muscle cells

Blood cells

Skin cells

Nerve cells

Bone cells

What makes you grow?

You grow because the cells of your body keep dividing into new cells. When you eat, your cells take in food and grow bigger. Then each cell divides and becomes two cells. Then each of the two cells divides, making four cells, and so on. As the number of cells in your body becomes greater, you grow bigger and bigger.

Lucy's trick isn't going to work. No matter how often she pushes on Linus's head, she won't be able to stop him from growing.

When did you start growing?

You started growing from just two cells about nine months before you were born. One cell, a sperm cell, came from your father. Another cell, an egg cell, came from your mother. The two cells joined together inside your mother's body. They formed a special new cell called a fertilized egg. This cell was the start of a whole human being—you.

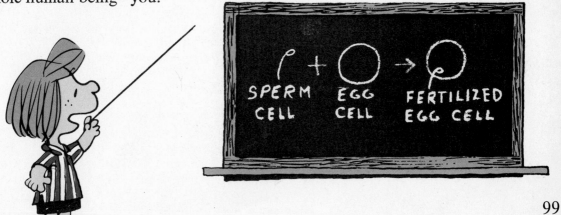

99

How does a fertilized egg cell become a whole person?

A fertilized egg starts out the size of the head of a pin. It settles inside a special place in the mother's body called the uterus (YOU-ter-us). Then the fertilized egg grows and divides in half. It becomes two cells that are just alike. Then these cells grow and divide. The new cells divide again and again. More and more cells keep developing. But after a while, not all of them look alike. Some are muscle cells, some are bone cells, some are nerve cells, some are blood cells. All the different kinds of cells that make up a human body are there.

About a week after the fertilized egg began to divide, the new cells start to grow into special body parts—brain, heart, and lungs, for example. After about two months, the developing baby has eyes, ears, a nose, and a mouth. It has tiny legs and arms, too. It has a complete heart that beats and sends blood through its body. But it is still less than an inch long. For seven more months, the baby keeps developing in its mother's body. It grows bigger and heavier. It looks more and more like a person. At last—about nine months after the fertilized egg began to divide—the baby is born.

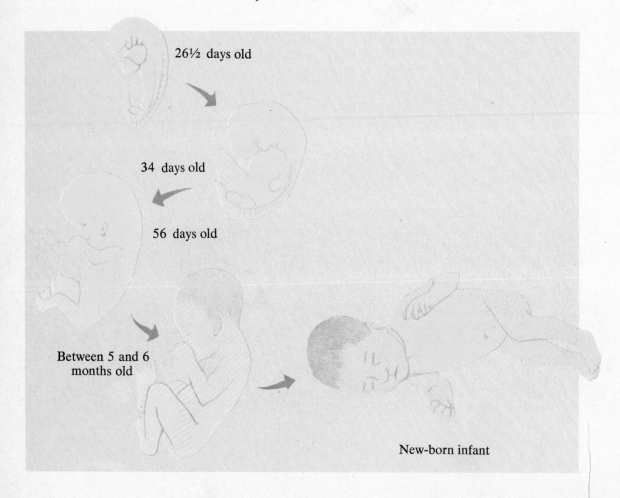

26½ days old

34 days old

56 days old

Between 5 and 6 months old

New-born infant

How big is a newborn baby?

When a baby is born, it is usually about 20 inches long, and it probably weighs between six and nine pounds.

How do twins start growing?

When two sperm cells join with two egg cells at the same time, twins begin to grow. These twins are known as fraternal twins. The two children don't have to look at all alike.

Twins that look alike are called identical twins. These start growing from just one fertilized egg cell. The cell begins to divide and grow. After a few days of growth, the group of cells separates into two parts. The two parts are exactly alike. Each part grows into a whole person.

101

Why do you have a "belly button"?

Before you were born, you and your mother were connected in her uterus by a tube called an umbilical cord. The cord was attached to you on the spot where your "belly button" is now. Everything you needed to live and grow—including food and oxygen—came to you from your mother through this cord.

After you were born, you no longer needed the umbilical cord because you could eat, drink, and breathe for yourself. So the doctor carefully tied the cord and cut it off as close to your belly as possible. But a tiny piece of the cord was left. This piece began to dry up, and it fell off about a week after you were born. A little dent was left in your belly. The dent is called your navel, or belly button.

When will you stop growing?

If you are a girl, you will stop growing when you are about 18 years old. If you are a boy, you may keep growing taller for a few more years. After you reach your full height, you may get fatter, but you won't get any taller.

Your Skeleton

FOR "SHOW AND TELL" TODAY, I WANT TO TALK TO YOU ABOUT YOUR SKELETON. IT HAS 206 BONES AND 32 TEETH.

Why do you need a skeleton?

Your skeleton is the framework of your body. It holds you up and gives your body its shape. Because bones are hard and strong, your skeleton also protects important parts of you, such as your heart, lungs, and brain.

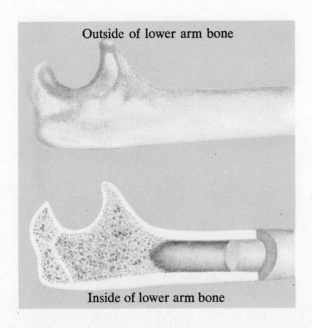

Outside of lower arm bone

Inside of lower arm bone

What do bones look like?

Your bones look somewhat like the beef bone Snoopy has in his mouth, but they are different shapes and sizes. On the outside, they are white and hard and strong. On the inside, they are soft and spongy.

What are the smallest bones in your body?

Three tiny bones in your ear, deep inside your head, are the smallest. The three together are about the size of your thumbnail. These bones look like their names—the hammer, the anvil, and the stirrup.

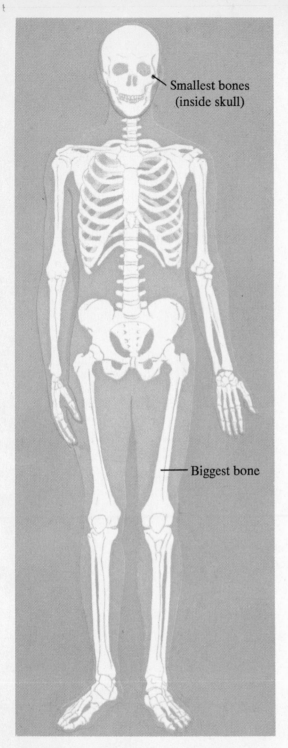

Smallest bones
(inside skull)

Biggest bone

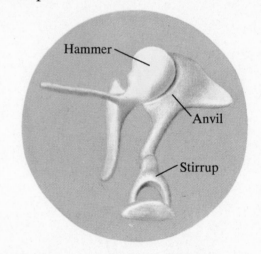

Hammer

Anvil

Stirrup

What are your biggest bones?

Your thigh bones, or femurs (FEE-mers), are the biggest. If you grow up to be six feet tall, each of your thigh bones will be almost 20 inches long.

Nearly half the bones in your body are in your hands and feet!

FOR "SHOW AND TELL" TODAY I HAVE BROUGHT YOU A LOCAL HERO!

THIS LITTLE FELLOW HERE BROKE HIS FIFTH METATARSAL WHILE RESCUING THREE AIRLINE STEWARDESSES ON RUNAWAY HORSES!

LISTEN CAREFULLY, FOR THIS IS THE WAY IT ALL HAPPENED...

INCIDENTALLY, MA'AM, ARE WE GRADED ON TRUTH AND ACCURACY?

Can your bones bend?

No. Your bones cannot bend. You bend your arms, your legs, and other parts of your body at the places where two bones join together. These places are called joints. You bend only at your joints.

Why do you need a cast when you have a broken arm or leg?

When you say you have a broken arm, you really mean that you have a broken or fractured (cracked) bone in your arm. In order for the broken parts to heal, they must be held in place. A cast does this job.

When a doctor puts a cast on a broken arm, he first places the broken parts together the way he wants them to heal. Then he puts layers of gauze bandage and wet plaster around the arm. The plaster hardens with the gauze and forms a firm cast. That keeps the broken ends of the bone from moving around, so that they can grow together again.

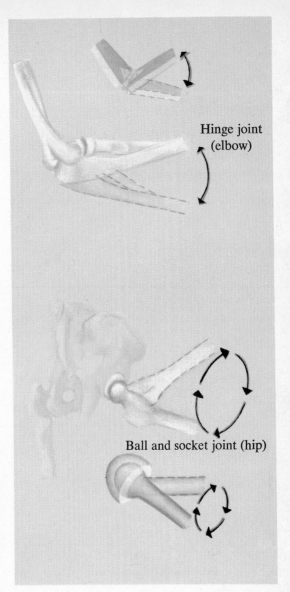

Hinge joint (elbow)

Ball and socket joint (hip)

GOOD GRIEF, CHARLIE BROWN! ANOTHER BROKEN TOE?

What is a "funny bone"?

A "funny bone" is not a bone at all. It's a nerve at the back of your elbow close to the bone. "Funny bone" is just an expression. When you hit your funny bone, you get a painful tingling feeling in your arm. As Charlie Brown can tell you, it's not very funny!

Why do your baby teeth fall out?

Your baby teeth fall out to make room for larger and stronger teeth. Everyone grows two sets of teeth. When you were about six months old, your first set of teeth started to come through your gums. These were your baby teeth. You had 20 of them, and they were very small.

These baby teeth did not grow larger after they came through your gums. But the rest of your body kept growing. So after a few years, your baby teeth became too small for your jaw. But in the meantime, a set of larger and stronger teeth were growing inside your gums. One by one, these larger teeth have been pushing through your gums, and your baby teeth have been falling out to make room for the new ones. The second set of teeth are called permanent teeth.

106

Do wisdom teeth make you smarter?

No. Wisdom teeth are simply the last four teeth that come into your mouth. You may not get them until you are a teen-ager or even an adult. Because they appear at so late an age, people call them them wisdom teeth. By the time you get these teeth, you should have grown pretty wise.

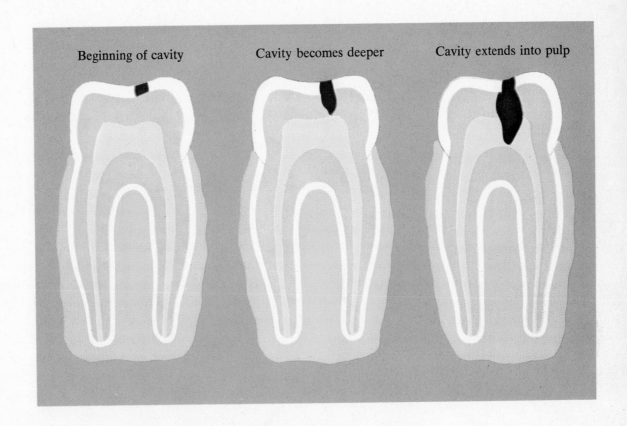

Beginning of cavity   Cavity becomes deeper   Cavity extends into pulp

How do you get a cavity in your tooth?

After you eat, tiny bits of food are left between your teeth. If you don't brush away these food bits, germs grow on them and start to eat away at the hard outside part of your teeth. The hole that the germs make is called a cavity.

How can you prevent cavities?

You can prevent cavities by brushing away the food left in your mouth after you eat. Then the germs will have nothing to grow on. You have to brush hard to get out all the bits stuck between your teeth. Brushing after every meal works best.

You can also help prevent cavities by not eating foods with a lot of sugar in them. Cavity-making germs grow best in sugar.

You should also visit your dentist twice a year. The dentist will check to see if you have any cavities. If you do, he will clean them out to get rid of the germs. Then he will fill the holes with silver or porcelain (POUR-suh-lin). The cavities will not grow any deeper and give you a toothache.

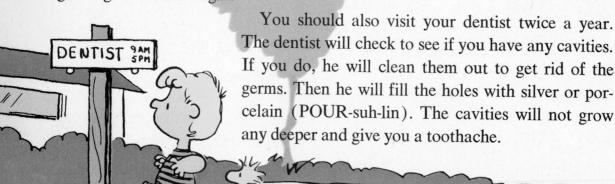

DENTIST 9AM 5PM

What causes a toothache?

When a cavity gets very deep, you will have a toothache. Inside each tooth is a soft, sensitive area with nerves in it. When a cavity reaches that area — OUCH! — it hurts!

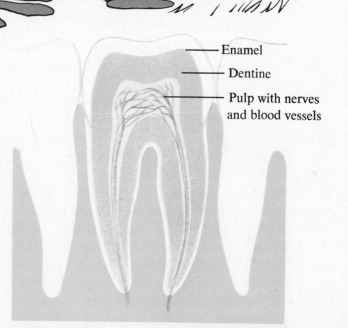

— Enamel

— Dentine

— Pulp with nerves and blood vessels

Your Muscles

Why do you need muscles?

You need muscles in order to move. A muscle is a bundle of cells that can tighten up and get shorter. Then it can relax again and go back to its normal size. When a muscle tightens up, a part of you moves.

For example, two muscles are at work when you bend your arm at the elbow. These muscles are called the biceps (BY-seps) and triceps (TRY-seps). Each of them is attached to two bones—one at your shoulder and one below your elbow. When you want to bend your arm, your brain sends a message to your biceps to tighten up. When the biceps tightens, it gets shorter, and it pulls up the lower part of your arm. When you want to straighten your arm out again, your brain sends a message to the triceps to tighten up. This muscle gets shorter and pulls your arm back down. At the same time, your biceps relaxes.

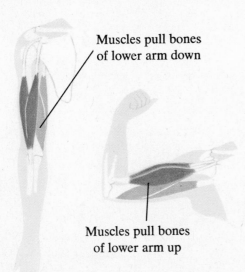

Muscles pull bones of lower arm down

Muscles pull bones of lower arm up

You can easily feel your biceps at work. Put your hand on your arm above the elbow. Now bend your arm. You will feel your biceps tightening up. Straighten your arm back down again. You will feel the muscle relax and go back to its normal size.

Why do some people have bigger muscles than other people?

The size of your muscles depends on how much you use them. When you do easy things such as sitting, standing, walking, or eating, you use only a small part of each muscle. But when you run, dance, play ball, or swim, you make your muscles work very hard. If you make a muscle work hard very often, it becomes much bigger and stronger. That's why ice skaters have large leg muscles and boxers have large arm muscles.

What is a "charley horse"?

A "charley horse" is not a horse at all. It is a kind of muscle cramp. If you exercise too much and make a muscle work harder than it ever has before, you may get a charley horse. If you do, the muscle will begin to tighten up when you don't want it to, and it will hurt. Resting the muscle and keeping it warm will help it to relax again.

Why do you shiver on a cold day?

Shivering helps to make you feel warmer. When you shiver, some of your muscles tighten and relax very quickly, over and over again. The muscles work hard —without your thinking about them working or even wanting them to. When your muscles work hard, you warm up.

If you play ball or run a lot on a cold day, you won't shiver. By exercising, you are already making your muscles work very hard. The exercise warms you up.

111

Your Skin and Hair

Why do you need skin?

How strange you would look walking around with your insides showing! Your skin covers your body, but it does more than that. It keeps many germs out of your body, and so stops them from harming you. It also protects the large amount of water that is in your body. If you did not have skin, your body would dry out and shrivel up like a raisin.

What are wrinkles?

Wrinkles are little folds in a person's skin. When you grow much older, you will probably get some wrinkles on your face. Attached to the skin on your face are more than 25 muscles. If these muscles don't get enough exercise over the years, they will become weak. Then they won't be able to hold your skin tightly to your face any more. Your skin will sag, and little wrinkles will appear.

Wrinkles can also be caused by staying in the sun too much. Too much sun dries out the oils in your skin. Without these oils, skin gets dry and wrinkly.

Why do you get "goose pimples"?

THIS GOOSE IS GIVING ME GOOSE PIMPLES.

"Goose pimples" are tiny bumps that sometimes come out on your skin when you are cold or frightened. If you look closely at the bumps, you will see a hair in the middle of each one. Attached to each hair, inside your skin, is a tiny muscle. When you get scared or chilled, each of these muscles tightens up and gets short. The muscles pull the hairs and make them stand straight up. The skin around each hair is pulled up, too. The result is little bumps. We call these bumps goose pimples because they look just like the bumps on the skin of a plucked goose!

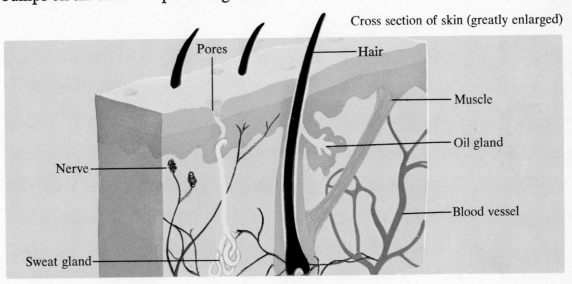

Cross section of skin (greatly enlarged)

Pores — Hair — Muscle — Oil gland — Nerve — Blood vessel — Sweat gland

Why do you sweat?

BOY, IT'S HOT TODAY!

You sweat to cool off. Your body is always making heat. When you exercise, your muscles make extra heat. On a hot summer day, the sun heats up your body, too. If your body did not get rid of some of the extra heat, your temperature would get too high. A very high temperature could kill you. So your body lets heat escape through your skin by sweating.

When you sweat, moisture comes out of your skin. The moisture has heat in it. It evaporates—disappears into the air—carrying the heat with it. Then you feel cooler.

113

Your skin weighs twice as much as your brain!

Why do people have different-colored skin?

The color of your skin depends on how much pigment, or coloring matter, you have in it. All people have some brown and some yellow pigments in their skins. But everybody has a different amount of each pigment. The amount you have depends on the amount your parents have. Because people have such different amounts of the two pigments, many shades of skin color exist in the world. "Black" people have a lot of brown pigment in their skin and not much yellow. "White" people have a small amount of each pigment in their skin. Oriental people have a lot of yellow and a small amount of brown pigment.

THINK OF IT THIS WAY PATTY · FRECKLES ARE A SIGN OF BEAUTY IN SOME CULTURES!

Why do some people have freckles?

Freckles are caused by the brown skin pigment called melanin (MEL-uh-nin). All of us have some melanin in our skins. If you have a lot of it, and it is bunched up in spots, you will have freckles, just as Peppermint Patty does.

When sunlight hits your skin, the skin makes more melanin than usual. So, although you may not have freckles most of the time, you may get them in the sun.

114

What is an albino?

An albino (al-BY-no) is a person whose skin does not have any coloring matter in it. Albinos also have no pigment in their hair and eyes, as other people do. Albinos have very pale white skin, very light blonde hair, and pink eyes. An albino's eyes are pink because they have no coloring matter to cover up the tiny red blood vessels that are in everyone's eyes. A person can have parents of any color and still be an albino.

What are fingerprints?

Look at the tips of your fingers. Do you see the swirls and loops made by the ridges of the skin? They form the designs that make fingerprints whenever your fingers touch something. Your fingerprints are different from everybody else's in the world. They get bigger as you grow. But otherwise they stay exactly the same all through your life.

Your fingernails are made of the same kind of cells as a bull's horns!

115

What is a wart?

A wart is a small hard bump that sometimes comes out on your skin. Many people think that you can get a wart by touching a toad. But you can't. A wart is caused by very tiny germs called viruses that get into your skin. If you pick on a wart and it opens, the viruses can spread to any part of your body that the wart touches. They can even spread to other people. Then more warts can grow —on you or on someone else.

Can you get rid of warts in a graveyard at midnight?

No. Many strange stories have grown up about ways to get rid of warts, but none of them are true. One story is that you can get rid of a wart by taking a dead cat to a graveyard at midnight—the way Tom Sawyer did in *The Adventures of Tom Sawyer*. This method is adventurous, but it doesn't work. There are only two safe ways to get rid of a wart. You can wait for it to go away by itself. It usually will, but only after a long time. Or, if you don't want to wait, you can have a doctor remove the wart.

What is blushing?

The way you feel can affect your body. Sometimes, when you feel embarrassed or ashamed, you blush. Your face and neck look red and feel very warm. Tiny blood vessels in your skin are getting larger and bringing more blood to the top part of your skin. The blood shows through your skin and makes it look red. The blood brings heat with it, so your face and neck also feel warm.

Why do some people have curly hair and others straight hair?

Hair is naturally curly or naturally straight because of the way it grows. Look at one of your hairs. It seems very skinny, doesn't it? But it does have some thickness. If the hair is a curly one, it did not grow evenly all the way through. Some parts of it grew faster than others. This caused the hair to twist around, or curl. If your hair is a straight one, it grew evenly all the way through. And so it did not curl.

Whether you have curly hair or straight hair depends on the kind of hair your parents and your grandparents have.

How fast does the hair on your head grow?

In a month, your hair grows about three-quarters of an inch! Even when you stop growing taller, your hair will still keep growing. It grows faster in the summer than in the winter. It grows faster during the day than at night.

How long can hair grow?

Very long! A man in India had hair that grew to be 26 feet long! But most people's hair never gets longer than 3 or 4 feet.

Your Brain and Nervous System

What does your brain do?

Your brain controls everything you think about and just about everything you do. Your brain controls breathing, seeing, hearing, and feeling hungry. It controls laughing, reading a book, playing the piano, talking, walking, and crying. Your brain lets you learn new things. Your brain also lets you remember things that happened three days ago or three years ago.

Feeling hungry

Reading

Playing piano

How can your brain control all these things?

Your brain is the headquarters of a giant message system called your nervous system. Your brain gets messages from every part of your body by way of special long cells called nerves. Your brain then sends its own messages back through the nerves to tell the different parts of your body what to do.

For example, suppose a fly walks across your neck and tickles it. Nerves from your neck send a "tickle message" to your brain. Your brain decides what should be done next. If it decides the tickle should be scratched, your brain sends a message to your arm to lift. It sends a message to your hand to scratch. So you lift your arm and scratch your neck.

Laughing

Crying

Remembering

What is your spinal cord?

Your spinal cord is a long cord made of nerve cells. It runs from your brain all the way down your back inside the bones of your spine. Most nerve messages pass through your spinal cord on their way to and from your brain.

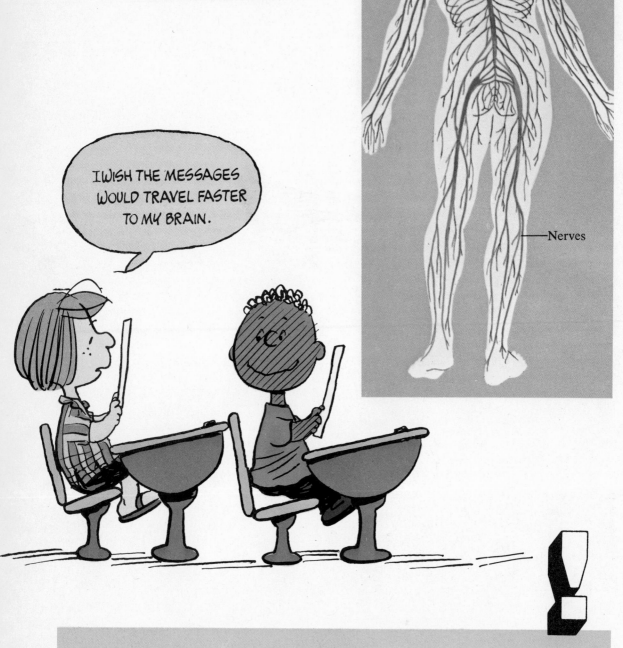

Brain

Spinal Cord

Nerves

I WISH THE MESSAGES WOULD TRAVEL FASTER TO MY BRAIN.

Some messages travel along your nerves at a speed of 200 miles an hour!

120

Why do you drop a hot potato?

You drop a hot potato before you even feel the pain that comes from burning your hand. As soon as you touch the potato, nerves quickly send a message: "Too hot!" This special danger message goes straight to your spinal cord. Right away, nerves in your spinal cord answer the message. They don't wait for the message to reach your brain. These nerves make you spread out your fingers so you will drop the potato. You don't even have to think about opening your hand. Then the message goes from your spinal cord to your brain. Your brain makes you realize that the potato was too hot to touch—that touching it caused you pain. You'll be more careful next time. Any danger message is answered by your spinal cord before it goes to your brain, so that you can act very quickly.

Do smarter people have bigger brains?

No. The size of your brain does not affect how smart you are. The brains of most grownups are about the same size and weight, although there are slight differences. It is very possible for a genius to have a smaller brain than a stupid person.

Your brain weighs more than a horse's brain, but less than an elephant's!

Which is smarter—a computer or the human brain?

The human brain is smarter, but a computer works faster. Computers can do only what people tell them—or "program" them—to do. They cannot think of anything new, while the human brain is always coming up with new ideas. However, a computer is very fast. It can, for example, solve in a few minutes a mathematical problem that might take a person many, many years to figure out.

What happens when you sleep?

When you sleep most of your brain and many of your nerves "turn off." Very few messages can then be sent to or from your brain. For example, when you are asleep you can't hear the TV in the next room. And if someone turns on a light in your room, you don't notice it. But while you sleep, many things continue to go on in your body. Your heart beats, you breathe, and you dream. Your body also replaces worn-out cells.

No one knows for sure why you sleep. Some scientists think your body needs a chance to rest and repair itself. Others disagree. Whatever the reason, you usually feel stronger and healthier after a good night's sleep.

122

During your lifetime, your brain may store
up to 100 million bits of information!

Why are some people left-handed?

Although most people are right-handed, some are left-handed, and a few can use one hand as well as the other. We say these people are ambidextrous (am-bih-DECK-struss). Not all scientists agree on what causes these differences. But many think this is the answer:

Each side of your brain controls the muscles on the opposite side of your body. In most people the left side of the brain is more powerful (dominant) than the right side. These people have better control over the muscles on their right side. If the left side of your brain is dominant, you are right-handed. If the right side of your brain is dominant, you are left-handed. If both sides of your brain are about equal, you may be ambidextrous.

Not very long ago, parents and teachers used to try and change left-handed children into right-handed children. Today scientists know that it is best for left-handed children to stay the way they are. Forcing them to use their right hand confuses the two sides of the brain.

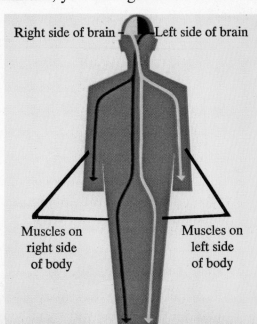

Right side of brain — Left side of brain

Muscles on right side of body

Muscles on left side of body

Your Senses

Why are you ticklish?

When you are lightly touched, special nerve cells inside your skin pick up the feeling. They send a message to your brain. Your brain can interpret or make sense of the message in several different ways. If your brain interprets the message as an unpleasant feeling, we say you are ticklish. If your brain interprets the message as a pleasant light touch, you are not ticklish. The touch doesn't bother you.

Why must you feel pain?

Have you ever wished that you couldn't feel pain? Well, you are lucky that you *can* feel it. Pain protects you and warns you that something is wrong.

For example, when you have an earache, nerve cells in the ear send a message of pain to your brain. Then your brain knows that something is wrong inside your ear. Your brain decides what you should do about the problem—go to the doctor, for instance. If you didn't feel the pain in your ear, you would not know that something was wrong with it. The trouble could get worse and worse, and your ear might end up badly damaged.

Why doesn't it hurt when your hair and nails are cut?

Hair and nails both have no nerves in them. Without nerve cells to send a message of pain to your spinal cord and brain, you can cut your hair and nails and never feel a thing.

How do you taste different flavors?

You taste with your tongue, your nose, and your brain. Stick out your tongue and look in the mirror. You will see little bumps on your tongue. Inside each of those bumps are about a dozen tiny taste buds. Nerves carry "taste messages" from these taste buds to your brain.

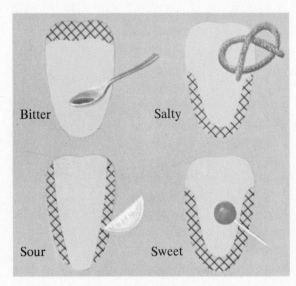

Location of taste buds

You have four kinds of taste buds on your tongue. The different kinds are in different places. In the back of your tongue you taste bitter foods. You taste sour things on the sides. You taste sweet and salty foods both on the sides of your tongue and at the tip.

But that is only the beginning of tasting. In order to taste the special flavors of foods, you need your nose. The smell of foods plays a big part in how they taste. That is why foods have very little flavor when you have a cold and your nose is all stuffed up.

Why do you sniff to smell a flower?

Everything that has a smell gives off a small amount of gas. You smell something when the gas touches special nerve cells high up in your nose. They send a "smell message" to your brain. Many flowers have a very weak smell. You must sniff to bring the flower's gas up to your smelling nerve cells.

How do you hear?

When sounds are made, they set up movements in the air. These movements are called sound waves. The outside part of the ear collects the sound waves. They move through the inside parts of your ear to nerve cells. The nerves pass the "message" of the sound waves to your brain—and then you hear!

What is your eardrum?

Your eardrum is a tough sheet of cells inside your ear. The sheet is stretched tight—like the skin across the top of a drum. When sound waves enter your ear, they hit the eardrum. The eardrum begins to move quickly—or vibrate—the way a drum does when it is hit. This vibration causes three tiny bones in your ear to vibrate, too. They in turn cause vibrations in a liquid that fills the deepest part of your ear. The moving liquid presses on your hearing nerve cells, which pass the sound message on to your brain.

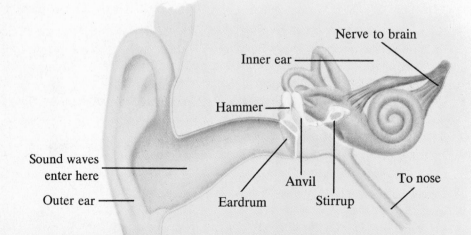

126

Is it true that your eye is like a camera?

Yes, it's true. A camera has a diaphragm (DIE-uh-fram) that gets bigger or smaller to let in the right amount of light. Your eye has an iris that does the same thing. A camera has a lens that focuses the light into a clear picture. Your eye also has a lens to focus the light. In a camera, the light forms a picture on film. In your eye, the picture is formed on the retina (RET-uh-nuh), all the way in the back of your eye. The picture is upside down on both the film and the retina.

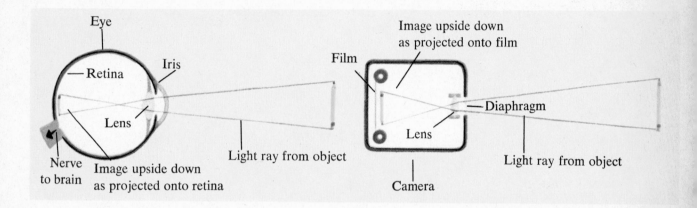

Eye: Retina, Iris, Lens, Nerve to brain, Image upside down as projected onto retina, Light ray from object

Camera: Image upside down as projected onto film, Film, Diaphragm, Lens, Light ray from object

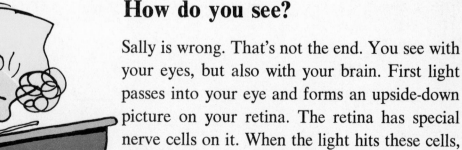

How do you see?
You see with your eyes.
That is how you see.
The end.

How do you see?

Sally is wrong. That's not the end. You see with your eyes, but also with your brain. First light passes into your eye and forms an upside-down picture on your retina. The retina has special nerve cells on it. When the light hits these cells, they send a "picture message" to your brain. Your brain interprets the message into a right-side-up picture—and you see.

Why do some people have to wear eyeglasses?

Some people need glasses because they can't see clearly without them. Three of the most common eye problems are being nearsighted, being farsighted, and having an astigmatism (uh-STIG-muh-tiz-um).

If you are nearsighted, you can see things clearly only if they are very near. If you are farsighted, you can see things clearly only if they are far away. If you have an astigmatism, things look blurry whether they are near or far. All three problems can be corrected with eyeglasses. Glasses help to focus the light properly so that you can see clearly all the time.

Why do so many grandparents wear eyeglasses?

When people get older, their eyes usually cannot focus as well as they used to. Things look fuzzy. So these people wear eyeglasses to correct the problem.

People have been wearing eyeglasses
for more than 700 years!

The normal human eye can tell apart about
‼ seven million different shades of color! ‼

What does it mean to be color-blind?

A color-blind person cannot tell all colors apart. Most color-blind people can
see shades of yellow and blue pretty well, but red and green look alike to them.
A few color-blind people cannot see any colors. They see everything in black,
white, and shades of grey. More boys are color-blind than girls.

What is ESP?

ESP stands for "extrasensory perception." These two words mean "awareness
outside the senses." Usually, we use our five senses to understand the world
around us. We see, hear, taste, smell, and feel. ESP means getting certain information about the world without using any of the five senses. Some examples
of ESP are reading someone's mind, knowing the future, and dreaming about
something as it happens many miles away. Some people seem able to do these
things. Scientists have been doing experiments for many years to find out if ESP
really exists. But so far no one has proved that it does.

The Food You Eat

Why do you eat?

Eating is fun, especially when you are hungry and you like the food. But you really eat to feed your cells, so that your body can grow healthy and strong. You eat so that you can have the energy to play and work.

Why do you get thirsty?

Your body has a lot of water in it—salt water. You must have certain amounts of both salt and water in your body at all times. When you eat a lot of extra salt, your body has too much salt in it for the amount of water. The same thing is true when you lose a lot of water. The thirsty feeling is a signal to drink more water and get the salt and water levels back to normal.

What happens to the food you eat?

You digest (die-GEST) it. That means that your body breaks the food down into pieces small enough to enter your tiny cells.

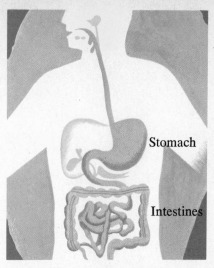

Stomach

Intestines

You start breaking down the food in your mouth. Your teeth chew it into very small pieces. When you swallow the food, it moves down a tube to your stomach. From your stomach it passes through a long, thin coiled tube called the small intestine. All along the way it is broken down more and more by juices —digestive juices—that are made in your body. Finally, in your small intestine, most of the food becomes a liquid. The liquid goes into your blood and travels around your body to feed all your cells. The parts of the food that you can't use soon go into a fat coiled tube called the large intestine. Then they leave your body as waste.

Why does your mouth water when you smell food?

Your mouth waters because the smell of food starts your digestion going. The "water" that comes into your mouth is not really water at all. It's a digestive juice called saliva (suh-LIE-vuh). There is always some saliva in your mouth. When you eat, a lot more of it flows in to start digesting your food.

But you don't have to put food into your mouth to start the saliva flowing. Just the smell of good food is enough. In fact, you can make your mouth water without even seeing or smelling food. Wait until you're very hungry and then think of your favorite food. Bet your mouth waters!

Why does your stomach rumble when you're hungry?

When you eat, food goes into your stomach. There, a digestive juice called gastric juice helps to break down the food. At the same time, muscles in your stomach start working. They cause the sides of your stomach to move. The movement churns the food and rolls it around to help break it down faster.

Because you usually have your meals at the same time each day, your stomach gets right to work at those times—even when you haven't eaten. If there is nothing in your stomach, all that churning can sometimes get noisy.

Why do you burp?

You burp to get rid of gas in your stomach. When you eat fast, you swallow a lot of air. Air is a gas. Too much air in your stomach makes you feel uncomfortable. Your body gets rid of it by forcing the air back out through your mouth. If you drink something with a lot of fizz in it, you may also have to burp. The burp lets the fizzy gas out of your stomach.

What kind of food should you eat?

If you want to keep your body healthy, you must feed it vitamins, minerals, proteins, fats, sugars and starches every day. You can get all of these by eating a variety of fruits, and vegetables; meat, fish, poultry, or eggs; milk or cheese; and cereal or bread.

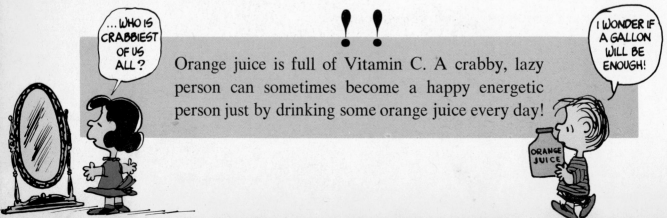

!! Orange juice is full of Vitamin C. A crabby, lazy person can sometimes become a happy energetic person just by drinking some orange juice every day!

Breathing In, Breathing Out

Why do you breathe?

You breathe to stay alive. When you take a breath, you take air into your body. In the air is a gas called oxygen that your body must have. Oxygen changes the food you have eaten into energy. Your body uses the energy to keep you warm, make new cells, move your muscles, and send messages along your nerves. You need the energy to do anything and everything.

What happens when you breathe?

When you breathe in, air goes through breathing passages in your nose. From your nose the air goes into a tube called your windpipe and then down into your lungs. There, oxygen is taken from the air. The oxygen then passes into your bloodstream. Your blood carries the oxygen around your body to all your cells.

At the same time, your blood picks up a waste gas called carbon dioxide from all your cells. Your blood carries the carbon dioxide to your lungs. When you breathe out, you get rid of this carbon dioxide along with the leftover air. Muscles between your ribs and under your lungs tighten and relax to pump these gases in and out.

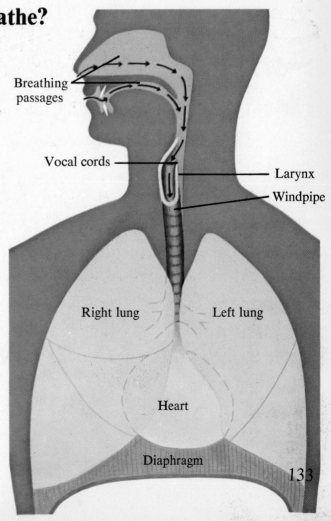

133

How do you talk?

Put your fingers on your throat and say, "Yes." Do you get a buzzing feeling on your fingers? The buzzing comes from the "voice box"—or larynx—inside your throat.

Inside your larynx are two vocal chords. When you speak, air comes from your lungs and passes between the vocal cords. It makes them vibrate—move back and forth very quickly. The buzz you feel when you touch your throat is your vocal cords vibrating. The vibration causes a sound. Your lips and tongue help to make the sound into the word "yes."

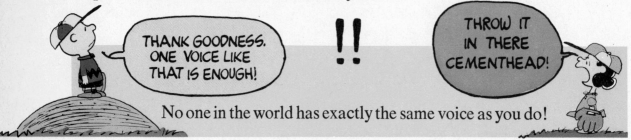

THANK GOODNESS. ONE VOICE LIKE THAT IS ENOUGH!

!!

THROW IT IN THERE CEMENTHEAD!

No one in the world has exactly the same voice as you do!

What is an Adam's apple?

An Adam's apple is a hard protective covering around the larynx. It looks like a lump bulging out of a person's neck. The Adam's apple is made of cartilage cells—special bonelike cells that also make up your ears and the tip of your nose. Everyone has an Adam's apple. But some Adam's apples are easier to see than others. Run your hand up and down the front of your neck. You should feel a small lump near the top, under your chin. That's your Adam's apple.

How did the Adam's apple get its name?

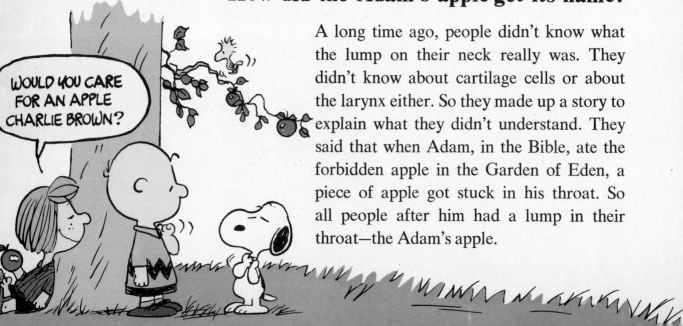

WOULD YOU CARE FOR AN APPLE CHARLIE BROWN?

A long time ago, people didn't know what the lump on their neck really was. They didn't know about cartilage cells or about the larynx either. So they made up a story to explain what they didn't understand. They said that when Adam, in the Bible, ate the forbidden apple in the Garden of Eden, a piece of apple got stuck in his throat. So all people after him had a lump in their throat—the Adam's apple.

Why do you sneeze?

You sneeze to get rid of something that is bothering one of your breathing passages. You may have dust up your nose, or you may have pollen—the powder that comes from flowers. A message goes to your spinal cord saying, "Get rid of it!" Your spinal cord then sends a message to your breathing muscles. They tighten and relax to make you suddenly breathe in and out with a lot of force—kachoo! And out goes the dust or the pollen from your nose.

When you have a cold, you sneeze because cold germs are irritating your breathing passages—making them sore. Sneezing gets rid of some germs, but it can't stop the soreness. So you keep on sneezing as long as your breathing passages are irritated.

Why can't you breathe underwater?

Your body needs to breathe oxygen. There is oxygen in water, but your lungs are not built to separate it from the water. They can take oxygen only from air. If you tried to breathe underwater, water would fill up your lungs, and you would drown.

Why can't you hold your breath for more than a few minutes?

Your body has a built-in protection against holding your breath a long time. When you stop breathing, you begin to store up carbon dioxide. If there is too much of this gas in your blood, a message goes to the part of your brain that controls breathing. Your brain sends back a message to your breathing muscles to start working. Soon you are forced to breathe again, no matter how hard you try to hold your breath.

Your Heart and Blood

Does your heart look like a valentine heart?

No. Your heart is not as pretty as a valentine heart, but it's much more valuable. It keeps you alive by pumping blood through your body.

Make a fist with your hand. That's about the size of your heart. That's about the shape of your heart, too.

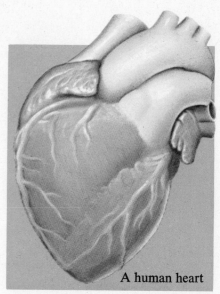

A human heart

WOODSTOCK, YOUR HEART RHYTHM TELLS ME YOU NEED A LITTLE REST. I'M GROUNDING YOU FOR A MONTH!

BLEAH!

What does your doctor hear through a stethoscope?

Lubb-dup, lubb-dup, lubb-dup. That's the steady rhythm your doctor hears through a stethoscope when listening to your heart. The heart is a muscle that is constantly tightening and relaxing as it pumps blood. We call this constant movement your heartbeat. The lubb-dups are the sound of the strong valves of your heart opening and closing as your heart beats. These valves act like one-way doors, letting the blood in or out of the heart. The doctor can tell by the sound of the lubb-dups if your heart is working properly.

How fast does your heart beat?

Normally, your heart beats about 70 to 80 times a minute. When you are exercising, your heartbeat is faster. When you are sleeping, your heartbeat is slower.

NO WONDER I FEEL TIRED!

Your heart beats more than 36 million times a year!

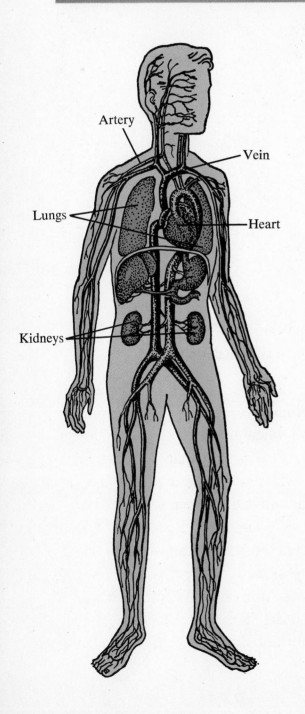

Artery

Vein

Lungs

Heart

Kidneys

How does blood travel around your body?

Your blood makes a round trip through your body in less than a minute, thousands of times a day. It travels through tubes called blood vessels. There are three main kinds of blood vessels—arteries (ARE-tuh-reez), veins (VANES), and capillaries (CAP-ih-ler-eez).

When blood is pumped out of your heart it goes into your largest arteries. These branch into smaller arteries, which branch into still smaller ones. The blood flows from the smallest arteries into your capillaries.

Capillaries are bridges between your arteries and your veins. They are the tiniest blood vessels, so small that you cannot see them without a microscope. Blood travels from the capillaries into tiny veins. These lead to larger and still larger veins. Finally, the largest veins take the blood back to your heart.

137

Why do you need blood?

Blood feeds your cells, cleans them, and works to keep them healthy. It carries food and oxygen to every cell of your body. The food and oxygen get into your cells by passing through the thin walls of your capillaries.

Blood cleans all your cells by picking up wastes from them. The wastes pass from your cells, through the capillary walls, into your blood. The wastes called urea (you-REE-uh) and uric acid are carried by the blood to your kidneys. There the wastes mix with water and then leave your body as urine (YOUR-in). The waste gas called carbon dioxide is carried by the blood to your lungs. It leaves your body when you breathe out.

Blood also protects you. It has special cells in it that fight germs.

How do your special blood cells fight germs?

The cells in your blood that fight germs are called "white cells." These are like an army for your body. They kill harmful germs that get into your blood. When a large number of germs enter your body, the number of white-cell "soldiers" grows. A lot of blood moves to the area where the germs are. The white-cell soldiers attack the germs and kill them. The used white cells and dead germs form the thick yellow liquid called pus. If the pus is inside a sore on your skin, it may leak out.

Why do you bleed?

A cut bleeds because it has opened some of your arteries, veins, or capillaries. Most cuts don't cause much bleeding because they open only the very small blood vessels. Because these vessels are narrow, blood moves through them very slowly, and comes out of them very slowly, too. If you should ever cut a large vein or artery, you would bleed very heavily.

If you lined up all your capillaries end to end,
you would have a string more than 16,000 miles long!

Why do people stop bleeding?

Most people are born with a natural protection against losing too much blood. As soon as a cut starts to bleed, your body goes to work to stop it. The blood clots—thickens—and stops flowing. Soon you will see a scab on the cut. The scab is nothing more than dried, clotted blood.

If you are bleeding heavily, you can help blood clot faster by pressing on the cut or by bandaging it. But that isn't necessary with a small cut. It will clot all by itself.

What are black-and-blue marks?

Black-and-blue marks are signs of bleeding under your skin. When you cut your-self you break open blood vessels and you bleed. When you bump into some-thing, you may also break open blood vessels. But since your skin isn't broken, the blood can't come out. It stays under your skin, where its red coloring changes to yellow, green, and blue. When these colors show through your skin, we say you have a black-and-blue mark.

How much blood do you have in your body?

If you weigh about 100 pounds, you have about seven pounds of blood in your body. That much blood would fill about four quart-size milk containers. If you weigh less, you have less blood. When you become an adult, you will probably have enough blood to fill five or six quart-size milk containers.

Why is blood red?

Blood looks as if it's solid red, but it's not. If you look at blood under a microscope, you will see that it is made up of several different kinds of cells. Only one kind is red. But this one kind gives blood its red color.

What makes your foot "go to sleep"?

Sometimes, after you have been sitting on your foot, you get a prickly feeling in it. That feeling means that not enough blood has been moving through your foot. You have been squeezing the veins and arteries so that blood could barely pass through them. When this happens, your blood can't carry the wastes out of your cells. Your nerve cells become "poisoned" with wastes. They aren't able to send messages to your brain. Your foot feels numb, and we say it has "gone to sleep." But when you get up and stretch your foot out again, blood suddenly starts flowing again. The nerves in your foot begin to send a lot of messages to your brain. You feel all the activity as "pins and needles" pricking your foot.

Keeping Healthy

What are drugs?

Drugs are anything you take into your body, besides food, that makes your body change. If the change mainly helps your body, the drug is called a medicine. If the change mainly harms your body, the drug is called either a poison or a narcotic (nar-KOT-ick). A poison will make you very sick or will kill you. A narcotic is a habit-forming drug. Once you have a lot of it in your body, you need to keep taking it all the time. Otherwise you may feel nervous, get terrible body aches, or have other problems. Doctors sometimes give small doses of narcotics such as codeine (KOE-deen) or morphine (MORE-feen) to patients as medicines. These narcotics are helpful because they can stop pain.

Other drugs that doctors consider helpful are aspirin and penicillin. Some drugs that doctors consider harmful are heroin (HEHR-o-in), a very dangerous narcotic that is illegal for anyone to use, and nicotine (NICK-uh-teen), a poison found in cigarettes.

Almost all drugs—medicines or not—have a very powerful effect on the body. If too much of any drug gets into your body, it can make you sick or kill you. It is against the law to take most drugs without a doctor's permission.

What are germs?

Germs are tiny living things, so small that you cannot see them without a microscope. Some are called bacteria (back-TEER-ee-uh), and some are called viruses. They are everywhere around us and in us. Viruses and some bacteria are harmful. If they get into your body, they grow very rapidly. Harmful germs can give you a cough, a fever, or the measles.

You can help protect yourself from harmful germs by keeping your body clean and strong—and by being careful who you share your straws with!

What is a virus?

A virus is a kind of germ that can cause you to get sick. Many viruses are so small that you can't see them through an ordinary microscope. You must have a very powerful instrument, an electron microscope, to see them. Doctors often know that viruses are in your body even if they can't see them. Special signs, called symptoms, appear in your body when it is fighting viruses. The lumpy, swollen neck you get with mumps and the high fever you get with flu are all symptoms. Doctors can often tell from symptoms just which viruses are at work in your body. And they can give you medicines to help you feel better.

Why can't you get the chicken pox more than once?

When you get sick, your white blood cells begin fighting the harmful germs in your body. One of the ways that the white cells fight is by making special germ-killers called antibodies. White cells make antibodies for each particular sickness.

If you get the chicken pox, your white cells make chicken pox antibodies. After you are better, these antibodies stay in your blood and keep killing any chicken pox viruses that get into your body. That is why you can't get chicken pox twice. You have become "immune" to the chicken pox.

What do shots do for you?

Some shots let your body make antibodies for a disease, without your ever having to get that disease. When your doctor gives you a shot for whooping cough, he puts a special liquid into your body. It causes your body to make antibodies against whooping cough germs. Then you become immune to whooping cough.

Sometimes your doctor gives you a shot of a "serum." Serum already has antibodies in it. It takes the place of your own antibodies and protects you against a particular disease.

If harmful bacteria have made you sick, your doctor may give you a shot of medicine. The medicine kills bacteria faster and better than your own white cells and antibodies can. Then you get well more quickly. So far scientists have not discovered any medicine that can kill viruses.

Will you catch cold if you get caught in the rain on a chilly day?

Probably not. You cannot catch a cold simply by getting caught in the rain. Viruses must start to grow inside your nose or throat before you can get a cold. Scientists believe that these viruses get into your body when you breathe. When someone with a cold coughs or sneezes, many virsuses escape into the air. If you are nearby, you can breathe in these viruses. If your body doesn't fight them off before they grow, you get the cold.

A chill from the rain may make your body weaker than it normally is. If some viruses are already in your nose or throat, your body won't be able to keep fighting them off. Or if you breathe in some viruses while you are chilled, your body may be too weak to kill them right away. Then they will grow and spread, and you will get a cold.

CHARLIE BROWN, YOU'RE REALLY PUSHING IT!

Why can you get many colds?

When you get a cold, your body makes antibodies to fight the particular virus that has come into your body. You will never get a cold from that kind of virus again. However, more than 200 different kinds of viruses can cause colds. So, if a new cold virus enters your body, you will not have antibodies in your blood to fight it. Then you will get another cold.

What are tonsils?

Tonsils are found all the way in the back of your mouth, at the top of your throat. You have one tonsil on each side of your throat. Tonsils trap harmful germs that come in through your mouth, and they make extra white blood cells to fight these germs.

When you get a sore throat, your tonsils will often swell up. They swell because they are working to help your throat get well, not because anything is wrong with them.

Until recently, doctors used to remove the tonsils from children who often had swollen tonsils and sore throats. They thought that the swollen tonsils were causing the sore throats. But now they know that the sore throats are causing the swollen tonsils. So they treat the sore throats, and they don't remove the tonsils.

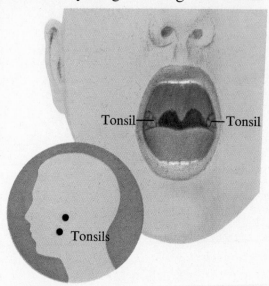

Tonsil — — Tonsil

Tonsils

What is fever?

Fever is a body temperature that is a lot higher than normal. It is usually a sign that you have germs growing somewhere inside you.

Your body is always making heat. Normally, a special part of your brain controls your temperature, keeping it at 98.6°F. When you feel cold, this part of your brain sends messages to certain muscles to make you shiver. When you feel hot, it sends messages to your skin to make you sweat. But when you get sick, the germs in your body upset this special part of your brain, and your temperature goes up. Certain medicines can bring the temperature back to the right level again.

THAT'S RIDICULOUS! YOU CAN'T TOAST A MARSHMALLOW OVER A BIRD'S HEAD!

YOU CAN IF HE HAS A FEVER!

Index

References to pictures are in *italic type*.